IN THE SHAPE OF A HUMAN BODY I AM VISITING THE EARTH

Cover design by Sunra Thompson

The editors wish to thank San Diego State University, *The Believer*, McSweeney's Poetry
Series, Maura Reilly-Ulmanek, Rachel Z. Arndt, Jennifer Minniti-Shippey, and Tamaria
del Rio. The publication of this volume is made possible by a generous grant from the
Edwin Watkins Foundation.

The object you are holding is a special issue of *Poetry International* #24. The following
poems, republished in *Poetry International*, originally appeared in *The Believer*: "Hustle"
(Jericho Brown), "Autobiography" (Michael Dumanis), "Kings" (Adam Zagajewski),
"Fatal Flaw" (Kay Ryan), "A ooooo" (Xi Chuan), "96" and "100" (Yu Jian), "The War Next
Door" (James Tate), "Fata Morgana" (Yusef Komunyakaa), "On Giving Birth" (Kathleen
Ossip), "Field Guide" (Tracy K. Smith), "No Opera" (Derek Walcott), "Hello, Brother"
(Zubair Ahmed), ["I once was a child am a child ..."] (Victoria Chang), "The Craft Talk"
(Rae Armantrout). All the poems herein appeared in previous issues, and are reprinted
here to celebrate the 25th year of publication of this international literary journal.

Poetry International is published annually at:

San Diego State University
The Department of English
and Comparative Literature
5500 Campanile Drive
San Diego, CA 92182-6020

You can find more information about *Poetry International* at:
poetryinternational.sdsu.edu

Printed in the United States.

ISBN 978-1-944211-07-3

2   3   4   5   6   7   8   9   10   11

www.mcsweeneys.net

IN THE SHAPE OF A HUMAN BODY I AM VISITING THE EARTH

POEMS FROM FAR AND WIDE

Edited by Ilya Kaminsky, Dominic Luxford, & Jesse Nathan

POETRY
INTERNATIONAL

—

McSWEENEY'S
PUBLISHING

Introduction

Ilya Kaminsky, Dominic Luxford, and Jesse Nathan

In the Shape of a Human Body I Am Visiting the Earth: Poems from Far and Wide features a completely subjective, but, we hope, valuable swath of poetry from near and far. Our aim was to curate a small but sharp collection—an assortment of poems with teeth, in the hope that every poem cuts deep (as they have, with gratitude, for us).

In this sad political moment in Anglo-American history, when nationalism runs rampant in both the UK and US, when walls are built and countries are bombed and banned, we believe it is important to continue the literary dialogue, no matter the challenges. One of our explicit purposes here is to bring together poets from the United States and around the world, often placing them on facing pages, in conversation. After all, the history of poetry is a history of border crossings. Great poets (Wang Wei, Ovid, Dante, Milosz, Tsvetaeva, Hikmet, Akhmatova, Bei Dao, Darwish) watched their people migrate by the thousands, and yet proclaimed, as Boris Pasternak did, that "poetry transcends all borders, smashing those borders."

English has always been a particularly absorbent and ravenous language, informed by the cadences and grammars of other tongues since its inception. Latin, Nordic, Saxon, French, Irish, Welsh, and Italian poetries seeded the ground upon which English verse has grown. These influences became prominent again when Modernist sensibilities swept poetry in English in the early twentieth century, a movement sometimes driven by direct (if often quite loose) translations of poetry from other languages.

Despite that internationalist turn, readers in the United States today remain all too unaware of the contemporary and historical writings of their peers from other language-cultures. In this country, many readers learn about foreign-language poets after they turn eighty-five and win the Nobel Prize. But the most valuable, potent conversation between literatures happens more naturally—continuously and organically—and not from a museum-like retrospective. Our thought was to provide a smattering of both the known and less-well-known, the contemporary and the historical, in a cocktail of topics, tones, and aesthetic orientations, a cocktail we hope may produce surprising new experiences for you, reader.

All poems in this anthology have been selected from work that has previously appeared in *Poetry International*, one of the oldest literary annuals dedicated to publishing poetry from around the world. The challenges of creating any poetry anthology are, of course, many, and those challenges become exponential when one may include any poem written by any poet at any point in history. We chose, if not exactly to ignore these challenges, then to take them with a Parnassus-sized grain of salt. Perfection or anything resembling "flawlessness" in art—much less in a multi-author selection of poetry from around the world—is as inherently impossible as flawlessness in translation.

Our goal instead became something like the opposite of comprehensive. In order to make what you hold in your hands as readable as possible (as opposed to yet another guilt-inducing door-stopper), we gradually honed the available material until we arrived at a collection that we felt was wide in its reach, but still elegant; unpredictable, yet cohesive.

In short, we aspired to create the book that we ourselves most wanted to read. We hope these pages provide you with some of the pleasures and edifications that we experienced while putting it together.

San Diego and San Francisco, 2017

Visiting
Malena Mörling

In the shape of a human body
I am visiting the earth;
the trees visit
in the shapes of trees.
Standing between the onions
and the dandelions
near the ailanthus and the bus stop,
I don't live more thoroughly
inside the mucilage of my own skull
than outside of it
and not more behind my eyes
than in what I can see with them.
I inhale whatever air
the grates breathe in the street.
My arms and legs still work,
I can run if I have to
or sit motionless purposefully
until I am here and I am not here
the way death is present
in things that are alive
like salsa music
and the shrill laughter of the bride
as she leaves the wedding
or the bald child playing jacks
outside the wigshop.

Grandmother

Valzhyna Mort

my little grandmother
knows no pain
she believes that
hunger—is food
nakedness—is wealth
thirst—is water

her body like a vine wraps itself around her walking stick
her hair is bee's wings
she swallows the sun-speckles of pills
she calls internet the telephone to America

her heart has turned into a rose—all you can do
is smell it
pressing yourself into her breasts
otherwise it's no good
it's a rose

her arms like stork's legs
red sticks
and I'm on my knees
and I howl as a wolf
at the white full moon of your skull
grandmother
I am saying: this is not pain
just the embrace of a very strong god
one with an unshaven cheek that scratches when he kisses you

Translated from the Belarusian by Katie Farris and Ilya Kaminsky

Night Feed
Eavan Boland

This is dawn.
Believe me
This is your season, little daughter.
The moment daisies open,
The hour mercurial rainwater
Makes a mirror for sparrows.
It's time we drowned our sorrows.

I tiptoe in.
I lift you up
Wriggling
In your rosy, zipped sleeper.
Yes, this is the hour
For the early bird and me
When finder is keeper.

I crook the bottle.
How you suckle!
This is the best I can be,
Housewife
To this nursery
Where you hold on,
Dear life.

A silt of milk.
The last suck.
And now your eyes are open,

Birth-coloured and offended.
Earth wakes.
You go back to sleep.
The feed is ended.

Worms turn.
The stars go in.
Even the moon is losing face.
Poplars stilt for dawn
And we begin
The long fall from grace.
I tuck you in.

Child
Jacek Gutorow

Joy thinks I'm on its side
when I run through a snowy field
but death keeps its eyes open
and looks into my right pocket
where a plastic airplane
flies and flies in a clenched fist.

Translated from the Polish by Piotr Florczyk

Infinite Little Poem
Federico García Lorca

To take the wrong road
is to arrive in the snow
and to arrive in the snow
is for twenty centuries to graze the grass of cemeteries.

To take the wrong road
is to reach woman,
who fears light,
who kills two roosters in an instant,
a light that is unafraid of roosters
roosters who cannot crow in snow.

But if the snow makes a mistake of the heart
the south wind could arrive
and as the air does not take notice
we will graze again the grasses of the cemeteries.

I saw two spikes of wax
that buried a landscape of volcanoes
and I saw two crazed kids cry as they pushed the pupils of a murderer.

But two has never been a number
it is an anguish and its shadow,
because it is the demonstration and is not yours
and it is the walls
and the walls are of the dead.
And punishment is by resurrection without end.

The dead hate the number two,
but the number two lulls women
and as the woman is afraid of light
the light trembles before the roosters
and roosters only know to fly over the snow
so we must graze without rest the grasses of the cemeteries.

Translated from the Spanish by Janessa Osle and Amanda Fuller

Tracks

Tomas Tranströmer

Two o'clock in the morning: moonlight.
The train has stopped
in the middle of a field. In the distance, lights from a town,
glimmering cold along the horizon.

As when a person has gone so deeply into a dream
she'll never remember she was there
when she returns to her room.

And as when someone has entered an illness so deeply
that all that were his days becomes a few flickering points, a swarm,
cold and scarce along the horizon.

The train remains perfectly still.
Two o'clock: intense moonlight, few stars.

Translated from the Swedish by Malena Mörling

The Pleasures of the Door

Francis Ponge

Kings do not touch doors.

They'll never know this delight: sweetly or roughly pushing before oneself the large, familiar panels—to swing it away and then watch it fall back, to hold in your arms a door.

The delight of clasping the porcelain knob of the stomach high up in obstacle; this body-to-body instant lifts the lid of resistance, the room's eye opens, and the body slips inside, adjusting to its new apartment.

In your friendly hand you retain it still, before firmly pushing it shut, and enclosing yourself—while the click of the sturdy, well oiled spring confirms.

Translated from the French by C. Dawson, J. M. Lagedrost, and A. Robichaud

A Longing for Forgetfulness
Mahmoud Darwish

Darkness. I fell off the bed deranged by a question: Where am I? I looked for my body and felt it looking for me. Looked for the light-switch but couldn't find it. Tripped on a chair, it fell and I fell on I don't know what. Like a blind man who sees with his fingers I searched for a wall to lean on and slammed into the closet. I opened it ... I felt some clothes, smelled them and recognized my scent. I realized I was in some part of the world that concerns me, and that I had split from it or it from me. I kept on looking for the light-switch to ascertain this insight. I found it: here's my bed, there's my book, this is my suitcase, and the one in my pajamas resembles me. I opened the window and heard dogs barking in the wadi: but when did I get back? I don't remember standing on the bridge. I thought I was dreaming that I was here and not here. I washed my face with cold water, made sure of my wakefulness. In the kitchen I found fresh fruit, unwashed dishes that tell of a dinner I had. When did this happen? I checked my passport: it seems I arrived today, without remembering that I had traveled. Did a schism occur in my memory? Has my psyche split from my physical being? Frightened, I called a friend at this late hour: I think I suffer from an illness of memory ... where am I? I asked. You're in Ramallah, he said. When did I arrive? Today, he said, and we spent the afternoon together in the garden. Why don't I remember then? Do you think I am sick or something? He said: Well, these things happen to patients who suffer from longing-for-forgetfulness.

Translated from the Arabic by Fady Joudah

Hustle

Jericho Brown

They lie like stones and dare not shift. Even asleep, everyone hears in prison.
Dwayne Betts deserves more than this dry ink for his teenage years in prison.

In the film we keep watching, Nina takes Darius to a steppers ball.
Lovers hustle, slide, dip as if none of them has a brother in prison.

I eat with humans who think any book full of black characters is about race.
A book full of white characters examines insanity near—but never in—prison.

His whole family made a barricade of their bodies at the door to room 403.
He died without the man he wanted. What use is love at home or in prison?

We saw police pull sharks out of the water just to watch them not breathe.
A brother meets members of his family as he passes the mirrors in prison.

Sundays, I washed and dried her clothes after he threw them into the yard.
In the novel I love, Brownfield kills his wife, gets only seven years in prison.

I don't want to point my own sinful finger, so let's use your clean one instead.
Some bright citizen reading this never considered a son's short hair in prison.

In our house lived three men with one name, and all three fought or ran.
I left Nelson Demery, III for Jericho Brown, a name I earned in prison.

A Roomless Door
Jane Hirshfield

I walked
past a house

I walked past
a house
I heard weeping

I walked past
my father's
house
I heard weeping

it sounded
like

a piano's 89th key

Tankas for Toraiwa

Seamus Heaney

I loved to carry
Her violin case, its nose
In air, its back end
Nice and heavy, the balance
Factored in and factored out.

*   *   *

Every time she placed
Her two thumbs to the two snibs
And opened the lid
She couldn't help a quick frown
(Disguised pleasure?) as she checked.

*   *   *

Then her brow would clear
And the sun disc of her face
Tilt up and brighten
At the tap of a baton,
At the tip of a baton ...

*   *   *

In the blaze-lined case
Emptied of the ingrown jut
Of the fiddlehead,
A lump of ancient resin
And a dirty chamois cloth.

* * *

The conductor's hands—
Big and out of proportion
To his skinny wee
Professor's body—always,
She said, "interested" her.

* * *

Fiddlehead ferns: why
When I think of them do I
Think: *Toraiwa!*
Because—surprise—he quizzed me
About the erotic life.

Autobiography
Michael Dumanis

Attempted avoiding abysses, assorted
abrasions and apertures, abscesses.

At adolescence, acted absurd: acid,
amphetamines. Amorously aching

after an arguably arbitrary Abigail,
authored an awful aubade.

Am always arabesquing after Abigails.
Am always afraid: an affliction?

Animals augur an avalanche. Animals
apprehend abattoirs. Am, as an animal,

anxious. Appendages always aflutter,
am an amazing accident: alive.

Attired as an apprentice aerialist,
addressed acrophobic audiences.

Aspiring, as an adult, after acolytes,
attracted an awestruck, angelic auteur.

After an asinine affair, an abortion.
After an asinine affair, Avowed Agnostic

approached, alone, an abbey's altarpiece,
asking Alleged Almighty about afterlife.

Ambled, adagio, around an arena.
Admired an ancient aqueduct. Ate aspic.

Adored and ate assorted animals.
Ascended an alp. Affected an accent.

Acquired an accountant, an abacus, assets.
Attempted atonal arpeggios.

Earth and the Librarian
Jean Valentine

At the library
she passed a tray with little
books of baked earth on it—

Take one,
and eat it;
It is sweet,
and it is shed for you.

How can I live?
said Earth—

Nesting Birds

Gloria Fuertes

The birds nest in my arms,
On my shoulders, behind my knees,
Between my breasts I have quail,
The birds believe I am a tree.
Swans believe I am a fountain,
They all fall down and drink when I speak.
The sheep step on me when they pass,
And on my fingers the sparrows eat,
The ants think that I am dirt,
And men believe that I'm nothing.

Translated from the Spanish by J. Minniti-Shippey, T. Katz,
A. Fuller, M. Romero, and J. Nargizian

Wagner's Dreams
Alissa Valles

For Rene Samson

Above the low roofs of the town of Bayreuth,
above its thick air and its slender river,
above the forests of Bavaria, Wagner
is flying. His sideburns flutter. He's asleep,
he's dreaming, Tristan's chord travels
painfully across the German earth.
Wagner's asleep, his strength has ebbed, no more
does he climb trees in the orchards of friends
or slide down their banisters; he's asleep now,
his ego subdued for good. Let him sleep,
let him inhabit his dreams, where he forgets
his years of poverty, his bastard's birth,
his embittered revolutionary pride.
Let him inhabit his dreams, the only place
where he defers to another human being,
shows Dr. Schopenhauer a "flock"
of nightingales the master has already seen;
his dreams, where he defers to compassion,
to the unity of wronged and wrongdoers.
His dreams, where he is finally reconciled
with the phantom otherness of Jews, where
he talks quietly with Mendelssohn,
calling him Du; where his apology

is applauded like a diva's aria.
Let Wagner sleep, let him dwell in his dreams,
don't let him out, let him dream his music,
where he finds belonging beyond blood
and longing tempered by form. Music, where
the sound of redemption is something fresh,
a drink of clear water, a young girl's voice,
a flute. Let him seek refuge in music, where
the sweating bourgeoisie can't flatter him,
where even King Ludwig's search patrol
won't track him down. Let him dream,
turn his portrait to the wall, keep the earth
firmly packed on his lips. Let him float
on the wings of music, across a continent
Beethoven explored and left to Mahler,
let him ride "continuous melody" home,
released from the will by grace, a free gift,
or beauty, the same: for the final chord,
resolving our pain, is not written by us.

from **Lovegreen**
Forrest Gander

That the trunk, submerged in air,
whirling leaves, thresholds-out. On the bark of
its leader stem, a black-capped
chickadee pins caterpillars and lacewings.
Its water-sprouts and spurs unpruned,
unbraced, the Yellow Transparent tree's
boughs release the girl open-mouthed
pumping her two-wheeler
across a meadow softly-furred
as a bumble bee, her plastic bag
pendant with hard apples
from one handlebar swaying—

Coffee cut with honeysuckle.
The unprimed pump won't give up its water.
Mosquito hawk clings to the barn wall's shadow.

Untitled

Tua Forsström

There is something about
the cabdriver's childlike
cheek which means:
that it exists.
That it really exists.
That it streams a nightly
music along the ice cold road.
Yes, there is a glowing point
somewhere for all of us where
rags and masks fall.
So that rags and masks
no longer existed.
There we are eye to eye,
ashes in rain.

Translated from the Swedish by Malena Mörling and Jonas Ellerström

Firefighters
Avrom Sutzkever

Firefighters attack me late at night,
like nimble acrobats
in a circus,
on long ladders
quickly shot up to me
on the sixth floor.

Firefighters.
Rivers on their shoulders.
Axes and helmets.
Ripping pieces of flesh from my innocent walls.
A mirror shatters. Repay me what you owe me: A bit of my face.
Crowbars.
Streams.
Pillars of the air totter.
Men stand below
holding an outspread net.
Screaming—
they're fainthearted—
I should take pity on them
and jump immediately.

And I,
on the sixth floor,
in a royal pose,
am immersed in the work of a poet from the 13th century,
astonished
that the firefighters
attack me at night

with axes and helmets and insolence,
burning with zeal not to let me burn.

Translated from the Yiddish by Richard J. Fein

Fitzy and the Revolution
Ishion Hutchinson

The rumour broke first in Duckenfield.
Fitzy dropped the shutters of his rum shop.
By time it got to Dalvey there were three suicides.
The mechanic in Cheswick heard and gave his woman
a fine trashing; but, to her credit, she nearly scratched his heart
out his chest during the howl and leather smithing.

The betting shops and the whorehouse Daylights
at Golden Grove were empty; it was brutal
to see the women with their hands at their jaws on the terrace;
seeing them you know the rumour was not rumour,
the rumour was gospel: the canecutters did not get their salary.

Better to crucify Christ again.
Slaughter newborns, strike down the cattle,
but to make a man not have money in his pocket on a payday
Friday was abomination itself; worse canecutters,
who filed their spines against the sun, bringing down great walls of cane.

You'd shudder to see them, barebacked men, bent kissing
the earth, so to slash away the roots of the canes;
every year the same men, different cane, and when different men,
the same cane: the cane they cannot kill, living for this one day

of respite when they'd straighten themselves to pillars
and drop dollars on counters and act like Daylights is a suite
at the Ritz and the devastating beauty queens with their gaulin

fragile attention gave them forever to live in a tickle, the whetted
canepiece, this one day, forgotten in a whore's laugh.

Suddenly these men filled Hampton Court square
demanding the foreman's head.
They were thirsty for blood and for rum.
Fitzy stayed hidden in his shop behind the shutters.
He heard one man say it was not the foreman's head they should get,
that would not be wise.
The man continued: it must be fire for fire;
the factory must be burnt down.

But the men murmured. They were afraid.
Someone made a joke, they roared,
and soon they were saying fire can't buy rum,
they were roaring money, then rum, pounding Fitzy's shutter,
shouting his name for him to set them on fire.
They grew hoarse against the shutters.
The sun had taken all motion out of their voices.
Fitzy could hear them through the zinc,
like dogs about to die, cried-out children, that dry rustle
you hear after the crop is torched and the wind bristles the ashes.
No men were out there. Only a shirring noise.

That was when Fitzy opened the shutters.
Their red eyes in charcoal suits looked up at him,
and with an overseer's scorn, he nodded them in.

Cavafy's Builders
Ghassan Zaqtan

I have a tune in the melody
with which I did not arrive
but it is my only gold
and means

It has the probablility of improvisation
the tenderness of verbs
and the solidarity of narration

As if secret builders Cavafy had awakened
were passing through the hills
and started digging by my pillow

Translated from the Arabic by Fady Joudah

To Xuefei
Zhang Shuguang

Where is your face? flooded by what?
New York streets?
your head, tilted to one side, your neck
can't hold the weight of ideas,
where's your face? you are so clumsy
driving in Brandeis, your wife is
making souvenirs for who? a company?
and your son? in China? Why
you chose this damned
career of a poet,
I can't say ...
Your father curses you, your father
I do not know, writes
in a cursive that's yours,
since you are his son and
are in America, and Allen Ginsberg
and John Ashbery
are also there and are beautiful, and you
are hot, but I don't know why
you chose this damned career as a poet.
Wind and your face, poet, is
blurry and strange, I don't understand how these lips
eat steak in a restaurant
if I see you I'll punch you and say Hey Buddy don't lick
your fingers, speak better Chinese, boy,
and I will drag you

from your wife's angry eyes to City Lights,
    San Francisco,
City Lights, my Charlie Chaplin. City lights.

Translated from the Chinese by Katie Farris with Ming Di

Shakespeare

Marin Soresçu

Shakespeare created the world in seven days.

On the first day he made the heavens, the mountains, and the abyss of
    the soul.
On the second day he made rivers, seas, oceans
and all the other feelings—
giving them to Hamlet, Julius Caesar, Mark Antony,
Cleopatra and Ophelia,
Othello and the rest,
to master them, and their descendants
for ever more.
On the third day he brought the people together
and taught them about taste—
the taste of happiness, of love, of despair
the taste of jealousy, of glory, and still more tastes
until they went through them all.

Then some latecomers arrived.
The creator patted them sadly on the head
explaining the remaining roles were for
literary critics
to challenge his good works.
The fourth and fifth days he kept clear for laughs
clearing way for clowns
turning somersaults,
and leaving the kings, emperors,
and other poor wretches to their fun.

The sixth day he reserved for administrative tasks:
he let loose a tempest
and taught King Lear
to wear a crown of straw.

Some spare parts remained from the world's creation
and so he made Richard III.
On the seventh day he looked about for something to do.
Theatre directors had plastered the land with posters
and Shakespeare decided after all his hard work
he deserved to see a show.

But first, tired down to the bone,
he went off to die a little.

Translated from the Romanian by Martin Woodside

Anne Hathaway
Carol Ann Duffy

> *Item i gyve unto my wief my second best bed ...*
> *—from Shakespeare's will*

The bed we loved in was a spinning world
of forests, castles, torchlight, clifftops, seas
where he would dive for pearls. My lover's words
were shooting stars which fell to earth as kisses
on these lips; my body now a softer rhyme
to his, now echo, assonance; his touch
a verb dancing in the center of a noun.
Some nights, I dreamed he'd written me, the bed
a page beneath his writer's hands. Romance
and drama played by touch, by scent, by taste.
In the other bed, the best, our guests dozed on,
dribbling their prose. My living laughing love—
I hold him in the casket of my widow's head
as he held me upon that next best bed.

The Women of Kismayo
Susan Rich

The breasts of Kismayo assembled
along the mid-day market street.

No airbrushed mangoes, no
black lace, no under-wire chemise.

No half-cupped pleasures,
no come hither nods, no Italian

centerfolds. Simply the women
of the town telling their men

to take action, to do something
equally bold. And the husbands

on their way home, expecting
sweet yams and meat,

moaned and covered their eyes,
screamed like spoiled children

dredged abruptly from sleep—
incredulous that their women

could unbutton such beauty
for other clans, who

(in between splayed
hands) watched quite willingly.

Give us your guns, here is our
cutlery, we are the men!

the women sang to them
an articulation without shame.

And now in the late night hour
when men want nothing but rest,

they fold their broken bodies, still
watched by their wives' cool breasts—

round, full, commanding as colonels—
two taut nipples targeting each man.

from Building the Barricade

Anna Swir

> To shoot into the eyes of a man
>> *In memory of Wiesiek Rosiński*

He was fifteen years old,
the best student of Polish.
He ran at the enemy
with a pistol.

He saw the eyes of a man,
and should have shot into those eyes.
He hesitated.
He lies on the pavement.

They hadn't taught him
in Polish class
to shoot into the eyes of a man.

Translated from the Polish by Boris Dralyuk

I'm Afraid of Fire
Anna Swir

Why am I so afraid
running down this burning street.

There's no one here
except flames roaring skyhigh;
and that bang was not a bomb
only three floors collapsing.

Naked they dance, liberated,
waving their hands
from the window caves.
What a sin to spy
on naked flames,
what a sin to eavesdrop
on breathing fire.

I flee this speech,
which sounded
on earth before the speech of man.

Translated from the Polish by Piotr Florczyk

Magnificat

Eleanor Wilner

When he had suckled there, he began
to grow: first, he was an infant in her arms,
but soon, drinking and drinking at the sweet
milk she could not keep from filling her,
from pouring into his ravenous mouth,
and filling again, miraculous pitcher, mercy
feeding its own extinction ... soon he was
huge, towering above her, the landscape,
his shadow stealing the color from the fields,
even the flowers going gray. And they came
like ants, one behind the next, to worship
him—huge as he was, and hungry; it was
his hunger they admired most of all.
So they brought him slaughtered beasts:
goats, oxen, bulls, and finally, their own
kin whose hunger was a kind of shame
to them, a shrinkage; even as his was
beautiful to them, magnified, magnificent.

The day came when they had nothing left
to offer him, having denuded themselves
of all in order to enlarge him, in whose
shadow they dreamed of light: and that
is when the thought began to move, small
at first, a whisper, then a buzz, and finally,
it broke out into words, so loud they thought
it must be prophecy: they would kill him,
and all they had lost in his name would return,
renewed and fresh with the dew of morning.
Hope fed their rage, sharpened their weapons.

And who is she, hooded figure, mourner now
at the fate of what she fed? And the slow rain,
which never ends, who is the father of that?
And who are we who speak, as if the world
were our diorama—its little figures moved
by hidden gears, precious in miniature, tin soldiers,
spears the size of pins, perfect replicas, history
under glass, dusty, old-fashioned, a curiosity
that no one any longer wants to see,
excited as they are by the new giant, who feeds
on air, grows daily on radio waves, in cyberspace,
who sows darkness like a desert storm,
who blows like a wind through the Boardrooms,
who touches the hills, and they smoke.

Every Riven Thing
Christian Wiman

God goes, belonging to every riven thing he's made
Sing his being simply by being
The thing it is:
Stone and tree and sky,
Man who sees and sings and wonders why

God goes. Belonging, to every riven thing he's made,
Means a storm of peace.
Think of the atoms inside the stone.
Think of the man who sits alone
Trying to will himself into the stillness where

God goes belonging. To every riven thing he's made
There is given one shade
Shaped exactly to the thing itself:
Under the tree a darker tree;
Under the man the only man to see

God goes belonging to every riven thing. He's made
The things that bring him near,
Made the mind that makes him go.
A part of what man knows,
Apart from what man knows,

God goes belonging to every riven thing he's made.

The Garden

Yves Bonnefoy

It's snowing.
Under the flakes a door opens at last
on the garden beyond the world.

I set forth. But my scarf
gets caught on a rusty nail,
and the stuff of my dreams is torn.

Translated from the French by Hoyt Rogers

Kings

Adam Zagajewski

> *I'm a student*

Those were days when I walked around a little hungry,
a little dazed, and desire spoke to me
violently. A little lonely,
slightly happy, a bit the actor of myself,
I listened to music, the music was wild,
I admired the Renaissance palaces,
I visited our poor kings
at Wawel Castle and tried to comfort them
and stretched the truth; for all that, though, they
put fingers to their pale lips
and counseled silence. It was winter,
snow smothered the flowers, and the voice
of destiny could not speak soon.
So it was. Woolen gloves. Amen.

Translated from the Polish by Clare Cavanagh

God's Insomniacs

Edward Hirsch

Those sleepless blurry-eyed mystics—
Cioran called them "God's Insomniacs"—
mortified themselves
in the arid and obscure night.

They were *spirituels, contemplatifs,*
voluptuous sufferers
who could scarcely see the stars
through the bitter light of their tears.

One of the saints never slept
more than two hours per night.
She stood up to pray
and nailed her hair to the wall.

One of the saints dipped her forehead
into a candle, another tasted the flame.
She said it would start raining roses
after her death, though it never did.

Their austerities enthralled you,
one of the lonely agnostics
lying awake at night and brooding
about the hole in your chest.

Fatal Flaw
Kay Ryan

The fatal flaw
works through
the body like
a needle, just
a stitch now
and then, again
and again missing
the heart. Most
people never bend
in the fatal way
at the fatal instant,
although they
harbor a needle
they shouldn't,
or, conversely,
some critical little
life-saving sliver
is absent.

Etching of a Line of Trees
John Glenday

I.M. John Goodfellow Glenday

I carved out the careful absence of a hill and a hill grew.
    I cut away the fabric of the trees
    and the trees stood shivering in the darkness.

When I had burned off the last syllables of wind,
    a fresh wind rose and lingered.
    But because I could not bring myself

to remove you from that hill,
    you are no longer there. How wonderful it is
    that neither of us managed to survive

when it was love that surely pulled the burr
    and love that gnawed its own shape from the burnished air
    and love that shaped that absent wind against a tree.

Some shadow's hands moved with my hands
    and everything I touched was turned to darkness
    and everything I could not touch was light.

The Eyes
Antonio Machado

I.
When his lover died
he decided to grow old
in the closed mansion
with his memory and the mirror
in which she saw herself one clear day.
Like the gold in the miser's coffer,
he thought he would save
all of yesterday in the clear mirror.
Time for him would not run out.

II.
And after the first year—
"How were they," he asked, "brown or black,
her eyes? Light green? ... Gray?
How were they, good God, that I don't remember?"

III.
He went out to the street one day
of spring, and silently strolled
his double mourning, the heart locked ...
From a window, in the hollow shade
he saw flashing eyes. He lowered his
and walked on ... Like those!

Translated from the Spanish by Rosie Berumen

Like Homer

Ani Ilkov

The maiden in the dark is always singing
in the early morning or the early evening
while the grannies cast around their lightning
and their teeth "Dear God!" are rattling.

Dinner has been served upon the table,
but mice don't seem to care, in a choir
they sing along enthralled, as they are able ...

One of them resembled Homer.

Translated from the Bulgarian by Dimiter Kenarov

Love III
Alicia Ostriker

Too late for mating season
what is the cardinal doing
all week flying between

the feeder outside my kitchen
and the hedge by the brick wall
where a female or is it a juvenile

waits with needy beak wide
yellow-pink inside—not cheeping but
vibrating its wings so fast

they blur like a hummingbird's
it's the same thing
girls do with their eyelashes

the adult male pecks some seed
for himself then gracefully swoops
to her low branch

and feeds her
gets some for himself
and feeds her again

all week this goes on
I am almost stoned
just from watching

A 00000

Xi Chuan

He never looks back, yet knows I am lurking.

He shouts: "Stop on the edge of the cliff, or your body won't withstand
the anger."

He turns, sees the purple aura rising above me. He shakes his head, and
the sun sinks into the trees.

He sees the devil's shadow behind me. (He must have witnessed
Badanxin's smile, heard the azaleas sing.)

August, you must avoid crows. You must wake up early in September.
You'll have a great future, he predicts, but mean spirits will block
your path.

Another man appears in the lane and the stranger vanishes. I fidget.
Could he be my fate?

We pass, brush shoulders; he'll catch me again in this maze of ruins.

A crow flies across August's forehead.

I close my eyes, and the crow sings, "Don't be afraid. Your body is not
yours, it is a hotel for others."

Translated from the Chinese by Wang Ping and Alex Lemon

The Unspeakable
David Gewanter

My student Charlie Bernstein,
strapping, curly hair, about to take a step,
  like Rilke's blind man
pondering, fingers at his lips ... he wrote poems

about flowers, hillsides,
the girls he would bring there, and I nudged him,
  "send your stuff to the poet
Charles Bernstein, he says language writes his poems,

he says, 'that these dimensions
are the material of which the writing'—:
  this guy should meet another
Charles Bernstein. Tell him you wrote his books."

Curse my tongue. The boy
never mailed them, but after he left school
  he was driving all night
through Texas, and a truck killed him.

    *   *   *

I met Prof. Bernstein once
(stooped, alive) and told him about Charlie.
  He said _____. And I answered _____.
Two dray horses champing at seeds and forage.

from **The Night Chant**
Navajo

After Bitahatini

In Tsegihi
In the house made of the dawn
In the house made of evening twilight
In the house made of dark cloud
In the house made of rain & mist, of pollen, of grasshoppers
Where the dark mist curtains the doorway
The path to which is on the rainbow
Where the zigzag lightning stands high on top
Where the he-rain stands high on top

O male divinity
With your moccasins of dark cloud, come to us
With your mind enveloped in dark cloud, come to us
With the dark thunder above you, come to us soaring
With the shapen cloud at your feet, come to us soaring
With the far darkness made of the dark cloud over your head, come to
     us soaring
With the far darkness made of the rain & mist over your head, come to
     us soaring
With the zigzag lightning flung out high over your head
With the rainbow hanging high over your head, come to us soaring
With the far darkness made of the rain & the mist on the ends of your
     wings, come to us soaring
With the far darkness of the dark cloud on the ends of your wings,
     come to us soaring
With the zigzag lightning, with the rainbow high on the ends of your
     wings, come to us soaring

With the near darkness made of the dark cloud of the rain & the mist,
    come to us
With the darkness on the earth, come to us

With these I wish the foam floating on the flowing water over the
    roots of the great corn
I have made your sacrifice
I have prepared a smoke for you
My feet restore for me
My limbs restore, my body restore, my mind restore, my voice restore
    for me
Today, take out your spell for me

Today take away your spell for me
Away from me you have taken it
Far off from me it is taken
Far off you have done it

Happily I recover
Happily I become cool

My eyes regain their power, my head cools, my limbs regain their
    strength, I hear again
Happily the spell is taken off for me
Happily I walk, impervious to pain I walk, light within I walk joyous I
    walk

Abundant dark clouds I desire
An abundance of vegetation I desire
An abundance of pollen, abundant dew, I desire

Happily may fair white corn come with you to the ends of the earth
Happily may fair yellow corn, fair blue corn, fair corn of all kinds,
   plants of
All kinds, goods of all kinds, jewels of all kinds, come with you to the
   ends of the earth

With these before you, happily may they come with you
With these behind you, below, above, around you, happily may they
   come with you
Thus you accomplish your tasks

Happily the old men will regard you
Happily the old women will regard you
The young men & the young women will regard you
The children will regard you
The chiefs will regard you

Happily as they scatter in different directions they will regard you
Happily as they approach their homes they will regard you

May their roads home be on the trail of peace
Happily may they all return
In beauty I walk
With beauty before me I walk
With beauty behind me I walk
With beauty above me I walk
With beauty above & about me I walk
It is finished in beauty
It is finished in beauty

Translated from the Diné by Washington Matthews

96

Yu Jian

A cold front is attacking the city
3 p.m. the sky is turning gray
Cold has gripped everything
Someone starts to be afraid of life
Someone loses interest in travelling
Someone pulls his coat tighter
but when a beautiful woman appears
even if it's just a glimpse of her back in the street
the controlling force loses its grip
life wants to live again
the traveler feels like taking off now
the Kunming man who hates cold weather
suddenly lets go of his collar
revealing his neck, pink from the cold

Translated from the Chinese by Wang Ping and Ron Padgett

Fire

Adrienne Rich

    in the old city incendiaries abound
who hate this place stuck to their footsoles
Michael Burnhard is being held and I
can tell you about him pushed-out and living
across the river low-ground given to flooding
in a shotgun house
his mother working for a hospital
or restaurant dumpsters she said a restaurant
hospital cafeteria who cares
what story
you bring home with the food

I can tell you Michael knows beauty
from the frog-iris in mud
the squelch of ankles
stalking the water-lily
the blues beat flung across water from the old city

Michael Burnhard in Black History Month
not his month only he was born there
not black and almost without birthday one
February 29 Michael Burnhard

on the other side of the river
glancing any night at his mother's wrists
cross-hatched raw
beside the black-opal stream

Michael Burnhard still beside himself
when fire took the old city
lying like a black spider on its back
under the satellites and a few true stars

The War Next Door

James Tate

I thought I saw some victims of the last war bandaged and
limping through the forest beside my house. I thought I recognized
some of them, but I wasn't sure. It was kind of a hazy dream
from which I tried to wake myself, but they were still there,
bloody, some of them on crutches, some lacking limbs. This sad
parade went on for hours. I couldn't leave the window. Finally,
I opened the door. "Where are you going?" I shouted. "We're
just trying to escape," one of them shouted back. "But the war's
over," I said. "No it's not," one said. All the news reports had
said it had been over for days. I didn't know who to trust. It's
best to just ignore them, I told myself. They'll go away. So I
went into the living room and picked up a magazine. There was a
picture of a dead man. He had just passed my house. And another
dead man I recognized. I ran back in the kitchen and looked out.
A group of them were headed my way. I opened the door. "Why
didn't you fight with us?" they said. "I didn't know who the
enemy was, honest, I didn't," I said. "That's a fine answer. I
never did figure it out myself," one of them said. The others looked
at him as if he were crazy. "The other side was the enemy, obviously,
the ones with the beady eyes," said another. "They were mean,"
another said, "terrible." "One was very kind to me, cradled me
in his arms," said one. "Well, you're all dead now. A lot of
good that will do you," I said. "We're just gaining our strength
back," one of them said. I shut the door and went back in the
living room. I heard scratches at the window at first, but then
they faded off. I heard a bugle in the distance, then the roar of
a cannon. I still didn't know which side I was on.

Fata Morgana
Yusef Komunyakaa

I could see thatch boats. The sea
swayed against falling sky. Mongolian
horses crested hills, helmets edging the perimeter,
& I saw etched on the horizon scarab insignias.
The clangor of swords & armor echoed
& frightened scorpions into their holes,
& the question of zero clouded the brain.
I saw three faces of my death foretold.
I sat at a table overflowing with muscadine & quince,
but never knew a jealous husband poisoned the Shiraz.
I laughed at his old silly joke about Caligula
lounging in a bathhouse made of salt blocks.
I was on a lost ship near the equator,
& only a handful of us were still alive,
cannibal judgment in our eyes.
I came to a restful valley of goats & dragon lizards,
but only thought of sand spilling from my boots.
I witnessed the burning of heretics near an oasis,
& dreamt of gulls interrogating seahorses, cuttlefish,
& crabs crawling out of the white dunes.
I could see the queen of scapegoats
donning a mask as palms skirted the valley.
I was lost in a very old land, before Christ
& Mohammed, & when I opened my eyes
I could see women embracing a tribunal
of gasoline cans. I heard a scuttling
on the sea floor. I knew beforehand

what surrender would look like after
long victory parades & proclamations,
& could hear the sounds lovemaking
brought to the cave & headquarters.

Just Married
J. Hope Stein

Husband is food. I mean good
or roof. Which husband? *Men,*
women and snowmen— Where ...
is my underwear? Husband wakes me
with licking cheeks. I make pillow
of husband's shoulder and husband.

Dousing the dishes topless for husband:
I souse the mugs and bowls with warm
lemon froth and bubble; I sponge
our utensils: spoon, knife and prong,
for food we will eat next Tuesday
and Sunday & Tomorrow; I scrub
& bristle & muscle the pig-headed pans
with sporadic splash and suds to skin;
I rinse & fill & rinse & empty & fill & empty
& fill & empty to the music of water on twice the dishes.

Husband puts his face in a bowl of afternoon
cereal and we sing: *Where, where is my underwear?*
In the phenomenal
sock project, I watch husband place lone socks
across the kitchen table:
could be inside a pair of pants or suitcase.

In the earth of blankets, I gladden husband by the glow of lamplight
    through the sheets.

(Where is my underwear?) The sky drools sweetly to the ear, the purring
animals in our bed.
Light snore, the seashore at night.

The War Works Hard

Dunya Mikhail

How magnificent the war is
How eager
and efficient!
Early in the morning
it wakes up the sirens
and dispatches ambulances
to various places
swings corpses through the air
rolls stretchers to the wounded
summons rain
from the eyes of mothers
digs into the earth
dislodging many things
from under the ruins
some are lifeless and glistening
others are pale and still throbbing
it produces the most questions
in the minds of children
entertains the gods
by shooting fireworks and missiles
into the sky
sows mines in the fields
and reaps punctures and blisters
urges families to emigrate
stands beside the clergymen

as they curse the devil
(while the poor remain
with one hand in the searing fire).
The war continues working, day and night
it inspires tyrants
to deliver long speeches
awards medals to generals
and themes to poets
it contributes to the industry
of artificial limbs
provides food for flies
adds pages to the history books
achieves equality
between killer
and killed
teaches lovers to write letters
accustoms young women to waiting
fills the newspapers
with articles and pictures
builds new houses
for the orphans
invigorates the coffin-makers
and gives gravediggers
a pat on the back
paints a smile on the leader's face.
It works with unparalleled diligence!
Yet no one gives it
a word of praise.

Translated from the Arabic by Liz Winslow

The Star Frago Mashup
Geoffrey Brock

Detainee was beaten from the third to the seventh day
O see can you say

Was beaten with cables with water pipes
O bright stars O broad stripes

Had holes bored in his legs with an electric drill
O our flag was there still

Large amounts of blood were noted on the cell floor
O dimly seen shore

Was suspended hands tied behind his back by his wrists
O seen thro' the mists

Was electrocuted was sodomized with a hose
O breeze that fitfully blows

Back showed what appeared to be bootprint outlines
O it catches the gleam it shines

Reasonable suspicion of abuse
O stripes O broad O whose

Recommend no further investigation
O Pow'r that hath made and preserv'd us a nation

You

Osip Mandelstam

You, with square windows,
Squat houses in rows,
Hello gentle,
Hello winter,
Petersburg, Petersburg,
A thousand hellos.

*   *   *

To stick in the instant
Like a fish,
Like a dead fish,
Like winter-picked ribs

That up through the ice
Upset the blades;
To sing flinging
Skates down skate-cluttered hallways ...

*   *   *

Once upon a time
In a time still near
A potter and his fire
Floated like a tiny pyre
Farther and farther
On the red-shadowed water.

Tested by darkness,
Wrested from darkness,
A simple cup,
A plain well-made plate,
Sold on the stone stoop
Of any street.

* * *

Walk, workboots.
Get going, goners.
Past the Guest Yard,
The fields packed hard,

Where the ripe mandarin
Peels itself for your pleasure
And a measure of coffee
Crackles ecstatic

In your hands,
Smuggled from the cold
And ground to golden,
Home.

* * *

Chocolate chocolate
Brick brick
House house
Sweet Petersburg!
Nuzzleblizzard.

* * *

And the living rooms
With their pulseless silence,
All the unplunked pianos,
Sunken chairs, mingled airs
Of science and séance
As the doctors are treating people
—or maybe feeding people?—
With the *Neva*'s deathless prose ...

        *   *   *

After the bath,
After the opera,
After the after,

It's all the same,
Whoever one was,
Wherever one goes,

The cluelessness
And the youlessness
As the last tram

Lets one in,
So warm the eyes
So easily close ...

Translated from the Russian by Christian Wiman

Sniper
Pandora

When you see them on a flag march
Repress your swelling bugs
No mortar shells, no hand grenade explosion
This battle must go on quietly
With a calm mind, in cold blood
With sharp shooting, trained hands
Hone your skills when the sun shines
Camouflage like a chameleon
Be immovable as a sleeper
Don't blink, don't doze off
Don't miss your chance
If necessary, play dead
Don't flinch, even if they walk all over you
Blame fate if they shoot you point-blank
To double-check you are dead
Life may end up in anticipation, in Lethe
There isn't much of a choice to make
For example ...
Five enemies are approaching
Five bullets are all you have.

Translated from the Burmese by Ko Ko Thett

Fisherman

Carolyn Forché

March. The Neva still white, crisp as communion, and as we walk
its bridges, steadying ourselves on the glaze, tubes of ice
slide from the gutter-spouts to the astonishment of dogs, some of whom
have not seen spring before, while others pretend not to remember,
and a woman bends over her late potatoes, sorting and piling, and you say
"in this house lived a friend of my father who was killed" and
"in that house lived another, and in this, a very bad poet no longer known."
We come to the synagogue and go in, as far back as a forgotten holiness,
where we are told you can whisper into the wall and be heard on the other side.
But the rabbi doesn't know you are deaf. We whisper into the wall to please him.
A sign in Cyrillic asks for donations, and in exchange we apparently buy
tens of matzos wrapped in paper. *There are only a hundred
of us left in the city.* While we are here, a fisherman waits on the river,
seated with a bucket beside him, his line in the hole, but in the last hour
water has surrounded his slab of ice, so unbeknownst
he is floating downstream, having caught nothing, cold and delirious
with winter thoughts, as they all are and were, and as for rescue,
no one will come. It is spring. The Neva white and crisp as communion.

On Giving Birth
Kathleen Ossip

That night

I was

full of

information.

Track 5: Summertime
Jericho Brown

As performed by Janis Joplin

God's got his eye on me, but I ain't a sparrow.
I'm more like a lawn mower ... no, a chainsaw,
Anything that might mangle each manicured lawn
In Port Arthur, a place I wouldn't return to
If the mayor offered me every ounce of oil
My daddy cans at the refinery. My voice, I mean,
Ain't sweet. Nothing nice about it. It won't fly
Even with Jesus watching. I don't believe in Jesus.
The Baxter boys climbed a tree just to throw
Persimmons at me. The good and perfect gifts
From above hit like lightning, leave bruises.
So I lied—I believe, but I don't think God
Likes me. The girls in the locker room slapped
Dirty pads across my face. They called me
Bitch, but I never bit back. I ain't a dog.
Chainsaw, I say. My voice hacks at you. I bet
I tear my throat. I try so hard to sound jagged.
I get high and say one thing so many times
Like Willie Baker who worked across the street—
I saw some kids whip him with a belt while he
Repeated, *Please*. School out, summertime
And the living lashed, Mama said I should be
Thankful, that the town's worse to coloreds
Than they are to me, that I'd grow out of my acne.
God must love Willie Baker—all that leather and still
A please that sounds like music. See.

I wouldn't know a sparrow from a mockingbird.
The band plays. I just belt out, *Please*. This tune
Ain't half the blues. I should be thankful.
I get high and moan like a lawn mower
So nobody notices I'm such an ugly girl.
I'm such an ugly girl. I try to sing like a man
Boys call, *boy*. I turn my face to God. I pray. I wish
I could pour oil on everything green in Port Arthur.

Fatherland

Mansur Rajih

Do not despair, my friend:
The light that shines on our land
will remain chaste.
We still have time.

Maybe next year, the year after—
it will be enough.
We will see
the new face of Eban

smiling over our lives.
This land is good
and its history teaches us
we must not despair.

This land is happy.
Look, see the girls
painting their cheeks?
This land is continuously giving birth.

Yemen is a happy country,
the people die standing tall.

Translated from the Norwegian by Ren Powell

from On Living

Nâzım Hikmet

Living is no joke.
You must live with great seriousness
       like a squirrel, for example,
I mean, expecting nothing above and beyond living,
       I mean your entire purpose should be living.
You must take living seriously,
I mean so much so, so terribly
that, for example, your hands tied behind your back, your back to the wall,
or in your fat goggles
       and white laboratory coat
           you can die for people,
       even for people whose faces you have not seen,
       without anyone forcing you,
       even though you know the most beautiful, the most real thing
           is living.

I mean, you must take living so seriously
that, even when you're seventy, for example, you'll plant olive seeds,
    and not so the trees will remain for the children,
      but because though you fear death you don't believe in it,
         I mean because living is more important.

Translated from the Turkish by Deniz Perin

Field Guide

Tracy K. Smith

You were you, but now and then you'd change.
Sometimes your face was some or another his,
And when I stood facing it, your body flinched.
You wanted to be alone—left alone. You waded
Into streets dense with people: women wearing
Book bags, or wooden beads. Girls holding smoke
A moment behind red mouths then pushing it out,
Posing, not breathing it in. You smiled
Like a man who knows how to crack a safe.

When it got to the point where you were only
Him, I had to get out from under it. Sit up
And put my feet on the floor. Haven't I lived this
Enough times over? It's morning, but the light's still dark.
There's rain in the garden, and a dove repeating
Where? Are? You? It takes awhile, but a voice
Finally answers back. A long phrase. Over
And over. Urgently. Not tiring even after the dove
Seems to be appeased.

More of the Same
Kary Wayson

Even with my mouth on your thigh
I want my mouth on your thigh.
At the center bite of bread I want the whole loaf
toasted, and an orange. On a sunny day
I want more sun, more skin for the weather.
I'm in Seattle wishing for Seattle,
for this walk along the water, for her hand while I hold it:
I want to tie my wrist to a red balloon.
I'm counting my tips.
I'm counting the tips I could have made.
I want the television on, the television off.
In the ocean, I want to float an inch above it
and when my father finally held me
like a stripe of seaweed over his wet arm,
I was kicking to get away, wishing he'd hold me
like he held me while I was kicking away. Listen to me.
I want to leave when I'm walking out the door.

from **Lamp with Wings**
M.A. Vizsolyi

to be a poet you must understand how
to install a window i'm not speaking
metaphorically anymore there are books
on this kind of thing they are so
uninteresting you will find yourself
writing constantly on everything having
nothing to do with windows & sure
you can make extra money on the side
but that's beside the point you can
start a journal call it broken window
or lead a workshop on how-to manuals
& when a famous poet-mentor asks you
what you've been reading you can smile
& say in-depth window repair &
you can wink at her & she at you

    *   *   *

a woman loves to see her man with his
dick out walk into the room & relax
on the couch his balls softly resting on
the cover i am building a ladder i told
her a ladder to my penis so you may climb
up to it & hang blue christmas lights
from it to the window to the table
& back again we will drink virgin
eggnog & watch it's a wonderful life

every time a bell rings my dick will
get hard & the wire will tighten
the window will open slightly the table
will move & a tiny angel
will fly out of my penis and sing out your name.

     *   *   *

i don't believe the old when they walk
by me holding hands how can they love
each other's bodies when the young
girl with breasts as soft and bouncy as
the breasts of stars walks past them in a tank
top they smile at her this happened
today i was upset i asked them about her
they didn't notice the girl i was
upset i asked if they had any
identification they looked down & shook
their heads i arrested them both they
were sent to separate prisons my name
is radko yakovich soviet guard
budapest october 15 1968

Village of Pulleys and Locomotion
Rachel Galvin

I trail my suitcase along the platform
the weight of the air
at the small of my back. In the old country

a man would arrive from afar,
give each child a whistle, and parade them
through the village, whistling.

What is this fury of forms, boarding trains,
handing out whistles to children?
Dear spigot, dear filtering film of rubber,

if this world is the only world,
Anaximander will go on shaking his sieve,
persistently sifting with an ear to the ignition—

striker of matches, your scent of cloves, your fire
rides the circumference and a vortex gyrates at the center.
There is the vermiform signature: *you may eat*

of this tree. Now the glorious propinquity, now
the rupture. A village elder goes on debating
with his god. Who can tell if he receives a reply?

In the old stories, if you whistled,
the light would come to you
out of curiosity.

Intermittent
Youssef al-Sayigh

Tonight
the nightmare was very condensed:
a dining table
a bottle of wine
three glasses
and three headless men.

Translated from the Arabic by Saadi Simawe and Chuck Miller

No Opera
Derek Walcott

No opera, no gilded columns, no wine-dark seats,
no Penelope scouring the stalls with delicate glasses,
no practised ecstasy from the tireless tenor, no sweets
and wine at no interval, no altos, no basses
and violins sobbing as one; no opera house,
no museum, no actual theatre, no civic center
—and what else? Only the huge doors of clouds
with the setting disc through which we leave and enter,
only the deafening parks with their jumping crowds,
and the thudding speakers. Only the Government
Buildings down by the wharf, and another cruise ship
big as the capital, all blue glass and cement.
No masterpieces in huge frames to worship,
On such banalities has life been spent
in brightness, and yet there are the days
when every street corner rounds itself into
a sunlit surprise, a painting or a phrase,
canoes drawn up by the market, the harbour's blue,
the barracks. So much to do still, all of it praise.

Soot

Ana Blandiana

What do you think when you see
an archangel blackened with soot?
Of pollution of pollution in space, of course.
And what else?
The habits of angels
to poke their nose into everything.
And what else?
Of stoves that start
to smoke, to stop up in the spring.
And what else?
Oh, if I really think hard,
it might be an archangel
who set himself on fire
forgetting that
he could not burn.

Translated from the Romanian by Martin Woodside

Shoes
Mark Irwin

Matthew Shepard, in memoriam

They cover the human foot. From the Old
English *sceoh*, akin to the German
schuh, from the Indo-European base *s(keu):*
to cover. The arch, heel, and sole.
The upper, tongue, and lacing. Some wore wingtips,
Oxfords, and loafers, while others sported
walkers or sandals as they left
their offices and homes in that quaint
mountain town. He was tied, naked to a fence,
then beaten. They stood on a ridge. Some, barefoot, lined
their shoes along the edge. Others wore them
on their hands watching the sky.

Cardiac Weekend

Constantin Acosmei

(there's no devil in me—until Monday.
I stand by the counter where
I get my change close my hand
into a tight fist and give way

a woman slaps a child
sucking on his thumb—
until the crowded tram arrives and I
stick my shoulder in her ribs)

Translated from the Romanian by Martin Woodside and Chris Tanasescu

Memory of France
Paul Celan

Recall with me: the sky of Paris, the giant autumn crocus ...
We went shopping for hearts from the flower girls:
they were blue and they opened up in the water.
It began to rain in our living room,
and our neighbor came in, Monsieur Le Songe, a haggard little man.
We played cards, I lost the irises of my eyes;
you lent me your hair, I lost it, he struck us down.
He left through the door, the rain followed him.
We were dead and were able to breathe.

Translated from the German by Monika Zobel

On Deck

Kwame Dawes

Deep down; deep, deep down, you know
you can't blame nobody but yourself—
all you got is your eyes, your body,
then comes the waiting. Most of it
is in the waiting; what you do when you are
waiting. You don't think of a ball
flying, you don't think of folks
hollering; don't think of those dusty
bases slipping by one after the other—
no, mostly you think of the next
ball; and the ball before; you think
if you think hard enough, go quick
inside deep enough, look at his body
long enough, you will know his daughter's
name, you will know what he's had
for breakfast, you will know what
his brain is doing, working out what
the next ball should be, how he is
working you out, sizing you up,
wondering if you are cocky today
or drunk or careless; you have been
watching him, the slope of his shoulder,
the way a mistake droops his head,
the nod and shake, nod and shake,
shake, shake, pause, then nod

between him and the catcher,
the grimace and scowl when a base hit
skittles past his feet; the wrong ball,
how he sends the next, no questions
asked, how he smiles, when it strikes;
you study this man and you know that
if you look hard, you will find
his rhythm, read him, and if you get it
right, tell him what to do next
in a language he knows, teasing him,
edging closer to the plate, dancing
back, crowding, giving space,
and soon you and him are one,
each pitch a song you have written
until that sweet fast ball, just right,
the one he is so sure about, the one
you told him would trick you,
that late diving thing to make you
swing late; that one, that lie,
that simple flame that you smash
over his head, high and long—
and you don't look at the ball,
you don't look at the ball, you look at him
and you can tell, he knows,
he knows, he knows.

The Cross of History

Nikola Madzirov

I dissolved in the crystals of undiscovered stones,
I live among the cities, invisible
as the air between slices of bread.
I'm contained in the rust
on the edges of the anchors.
In the whirlwind I am a child
beginning to believe in living gods.
I'm the equivalent of the migrant birds
that are always returning, never departing.
I want to exist among the continuous verbs,
in the roots that sleep
among the foundations of the first houses.
In death I want to be
a soldier of undiscovered innocence,
crucified by history
on a glass cross through which
in the distance flowers can be seen.

Translated from the Macedonian by Peggy Reid and Graham W. Reid

Veronica's Veil
Tomaž Šalamun

In the valley
bombs are falling on the town.
A bee is tangled in the hair above my neck!

Translated from the Slovenian by Brian Henry

The Chinese Drawers
Yan Li

I pull out the Chinese drawers, one by one,
take a look at the years that I lived through;
in one drawer, those texts of
underground poems used to wrench themselves;
now, in the quiet, I can hear
the sounds of their retirement.

In another drawer
are a few grain coupons which are already antiques;
from the day they became obsolete,
I knew, even though they were cultural treasures,
they never had pride
for these crops from this land.

In another drawer
are two Red Guard bands,
one rusty fifty-percent steel watch,
and a couple of photos from the April 5, 1976
memorial in Tiananmen Square—
they all have the somber quiet after sacrifice.

The drawers, the Chinese drawers:
even pulling them out
from the bodies of the *five evil breeds*—
a Red Book must be in there.

Translated from the Chinese by Arthur Sze

Under the Floorboards

Rachel Hadas

Outside Bridgeport, the gold of afternoon
broke through clouds and factory chimneys. Brick
warehouses, pylons glowed
with late September light.
The blond young woman sitting next to me
was taking notes in a copy of *Beloved*

and skimmed from my light sleep, a dream came back:
two blond little sisters in a barn.
Trespassing, hiding in the hayloft,
I overheard them weeping.
The dream was so close to the surface
it almost bumped its head on the dusty floorboards.

A Prayer in Nineteen Forty-Three
Israel Emiot

For H. Lang
(Kazakhstan, war years)

Good God, look I'm poor, and trip over myself,
and my child wears shoes three times his size,
and plays with children, falls, and runs crying to me,
as I to you—with and without a reason.

I know all prayers crown you in gold
and address the most exquisite words to you;
still, don't insult the prayer of a child, who just wants
his own bed, and has to sleep fourth on the ground.

Your song—the day—I read and admire daily;
I still marvel at your last verse—your sunset,
but when I want to praise you my hands fail me!
Oh do not punish me, even my shirt is borrowed.

Wisdom tells me man is insignificant,
and earth the least of all your spheres;
still, do not punish me; listen to the lament
of a child who sleeps fourth on the ground.

Translated from the Yiddish by Leah Zazulyer

Hello, Brother

Zubair Ahmed

I pick up an earthworm
And you shoot it with a rifle.
Mom screams at us
But we don't listen.
She fed us expired milk this morning.
Sometimes in these Bengali summers
When dust sticks to our skins
And the crows shit on our heads
We bond like hydrocarbons,
Set mosquitoes on fire
And eat berries whose names we can't remember.
We ride our bikes like metal antelopes
Like drunken sparrows.
We play cricket under the monsoon clouds
And you bowl a perfect leg-spinner.
It starts to rain
So I shoot down a cloud.
We take it back to Mom
Who kisses our ears and pokes our eyes—
She does that.
We get ready for bed
With our usual battles,
And you fall asleep
Not knowing I slid the alarm clock
Under your pillow,
Set for 3:17 a.m.

["I once was a child am a child ... "]
Victoria Chang

I once was a child am a child am someone's child not my mother's not
my father's the boss gave us special treatment treatment for something

special a lollipop or a sticker glitter from the toy box the better we did
the better the prize one year everyone was fired everyone fired but me

one year my father lost his words to a stroke a stroke of bad luck stuck
his words used to be so many his words fired him let him go without

notice can they do that can she do that yes she can in this land she can
once we sang songs around a piano *this land is your land this land is my land*

someone always owns the land in this land someone who owns the land
owns the buildings on the land the people in the buildings unless an

earthquake sucks the land in like a long noodle

Between the Sultan and His Statue

Youssef al-Sayigh

A wily sculptor
Cut several pounds off the sultan's figure
And added several pounds to the statue's.
When day broke,
The people said:
We've been taken in!
Of the two bodies on the veranda,
We no longer can tell
Which one is the statue
And which is the sultan

Translated from the Arabic by Slaam Yousif and Brenda Hillman

The Craft Talk
Rae Armantrout

So that the best thing you could do, it seemed, was climb inside the
machine that was language and feel what it wanted or was capable
of doing at any point, steering only occasionally.

The best thing was to let language speak its piece while standing
inside it—not like a knight in armor exactly, not like a mascot in a
chicken suit.

The best thing was to create in the reader or listener an uncertainty
as to where the voice she heard was coming from so as to frighten
her a little.

Why should I want to frighten her?

At the Seoul Writers' Festival

Peter Campion

Riot police hustle in shield formation
past the American Embassy while we chat.
From the tour bus it seems pure spectacle.
We pass round soju in a thermos cap.

One row back the Korean student aide
prods the Filipino about his girlfriend:
"How does she look like?"
                          She cajoles him

for a photo.
                   Though on leaflets tomorrow
we'll see the nightsticked demonstrators dripping

blood on the pavement. And another aide
will tell me, gently: "It's not you we hate."

Right now, only the tubular glow of the bus.
Digital blips on the window. And English:

"How does she look like?
                    O ... beautiful."

Kinesthetic Sketches of the Dead
Eleni Sikelianos

Someone photographs his hands trembling in black air, radiating
    electricity & light

Balsa wood configurations are nailed to the legs to show which muscles
    move as he pedals
These are ghost muscles, limned in calcified lightning.
These are ghost hands, throwing off sparks.
These are ghost bikes.
For my father is always moving through the dark.

(The dead are caught in our studies of motion.)

I Know the Truth

Marina Tsvetaeva

I know the truth! Enough of the old truth—out!
No need people, with so many people on earth, to struggle.
It is evening—see—it is nearly night.
What speaks to you—poets, lovers, generals?

The wind bows low, the earth bathes in dew
and soon sky, starry blizzard will rest.
And under soil, soon sleep, we all will,
who never, on earth, let each other sleep.

Translated from the Russian by Lisa Wujnovich

Shed

Atsuro Riley

—But roughly but adequately it can shelter

In which she whomped
and tamped the earth to make a floor.

Beat a rhythm-rain
of brunts with oar and haft.

Gagged raw wallboards
(gaps and cracks) with chiggermoss with oyster-sacks.

Would some nights leak
a howl.

Rough-rigged a roof
(*some type of sail?*) from linoleum-scrimp and plastic.

Hacked a (splintery) hole
but hung no door.

Through which I'm put
more nights than not—*could I be the flickering in her structure.*

Would some nights leak
a howl (a count) a whistling-through.

I'm coiled inside
this shape she wracked and made.

Bare Feet

Tristan Tzara

what is this consciousness
that streams from man to man
prolongs the light
of sails where the mobile
weather of dreams
swells on air lanterns

a rooftop with clenched teeth
dances on your head
you work on locks
and in those crocheted flowers
you find the stitch
of clay
but no door opens
no lamp lurks
on the shifting salts
that the she-wolves of the evening
harry with their demands
at the bridge's step

the ports are dead
the night is drunk
up to the dregs of memories
no one passes through here
eyes of infinite ash
these i know
i count on fingers
the beauty of your lashes
the palms the storms

the cool water temples
composed in my hand

when the shadow discovered
the nakedness of your voice
in the little cottages
covered in scales
paths of solitude
solitude of the metal grate
cold muzzle where the tales
have chained themselves to the gold of the horizon
have pushed the designs of man
past cruel corners
there was a rustling a light touch
and the sure thing ahead of you
weighed the harvest
of mud and poverty
switchbacks of insomnia

not a muscle
not a comma
not an insect
nothing but the disasters
restless in the gulf's mouth
and the salt of the vivisection
on the edge of waking
i sang i bit the hook
of what i know
i rode alongside my doubts
i emptied my pockets
i gambled my years

Translated from the French by Heather Green

from A Love Note to a Brothel

Ikkyū Sōjun

A monk up in the tower and the whores around me sing:
Kiss me fuck me tear my heart awake.
Never forsake this body, this bundle of flames.

Translated from the Japanese by Jason Lester

Barbara

Jacques Prévert

You remember Barbara
It rained without ceasing on Brest that day
You came smiling
Flushed enraptured streaming
With rain
You remember Barbara
It rained without ceasing on Brest that day
I crossed Rue de Siam
I saw you smiling
And I was smiling
You remember
I did not know you
And you did not know me
Remember
Remember that day
Don't forget
A man took cover under a porch
And shouted your name
Barbara
And you ran to him in the rain
Drenched ravished blushing
You threw yourself into his arms
Don't forget that
Don't mind if I call you darling
I say that to everyone I love
Even if I've seen them only once

I say that to all lovers
Even if I don't know them
Remember Barbara
Remember
That wise and happy rain
On your happy face
On that happy city
Rain on the sea
On the arsenal
On the boat bound for Ushant
Oh Barbara
War is such bullshit
Now what's happened to you
Under this iron rain
Of fire steel blood
And whoever held you in his arms
Lovingly
Is he alive or dead or disappeared
Oh Barbara
It rains without ceasing on Brest
As it rained before
But this is not the same
Everything's in ruins
It is a terrible rain of mourning and despair
No longer a storm
Of iron steel and blood
Simply clouds
That die like dogs
Dogs that disappear
Under water in Brest

And rot washed far away
Far away from Brest
Where nothing at all remains.

Adapted from the French by B.H. Boston

Multiple Perplexity

Yannis Ritsos

He stood erect on the roof. "Now I'll jump," he shrieked.
The people below, motionless, held their breath. He made
a graceful motion—preparing to leap—then turned
and, with his back to them, descended the ladder quietly. For a few seconds
the people, ambivalent, laughed, got irritated, and at last applauded.
Only the two women looked elsewhere. The third was missing.

Translated from the Greek by Minas Savvas

The Snow Has Transformed the World Into a Cemetery

Roberto Juarroz

The snow has turned the world into a cemetery
but the world was already a cemetery,
and the snow only has come to announce it.

The snow has come only to point out,
with its slender and jointless finger,
the real and scandalous protagonist.

The snow is a fallen angel,
an angel who has lost patience.

Translated from the Spanish by J. Minniti-Shippey,
T. Katz, J. Nargizian, A. Fuller, and M. Romero

Crying With Glasses On
Eric McHenry

It's such a grownup thing to do.
Like renting tap shoes to perform
for no one in an electrical storm.
What's wrong with you?

Remove your spectacles and cry,
already. If there's rain
on your side of the windowpane
you're probably the sky.

What's the intention of a tear
if not to lubricate and cleanse?
I'll tell you: a corrective lens
is making things too clear.

In college I could see the future
coming and would often
pop out my contacts first, to soften
its least attractive feature.

If you'll just give it half an hour,
grief will discover
you drawing steam-roses in the shower,
and join you, like a lover.

Symphony No. 2
Daniil Kharms

Anton Mikhailovich spat, said "gosh," spat again, said "gosh" again, spat again, said "gosh" again, and left. To hell with him. Let me tell you about Ilya Pavlovich.

Ilya Pavlovich was born in 1893 in Constantinople. When he was a small boy, his family moved to Petersburg, where he graduated from a German school on Kirochnaya Street. Then he worked in some kind of a store, then he did something else, and right before the revolution he immigrated. To hell with him. Let me tell you about Anna Ignatievna.

It's not that easy to talk about Anna Ignatievna. First of all, I know almost nothing about her. Secondly, I have just fallen off the chair and have forgotten what I was about to say. Let me tell you about myself.

I'm tall, not unintelligent; I dress elegantly and tastefully; I don't drink, don't gamble, but I do like ladies. And ladies don't avoid me. No, they even like it when I go out with them. Seraphima Izmailovna has been inviting me to her place, and Zinaida Yakovlevna has mentioned that she is always happy to see me.

I did have a funny incident with Marina Petrovna that I'd like to tell you about. Quite an ordinary thing, but still rather funny, since, because of me, Marina Petrovna turned completely bald, like a palm of a hand. This is how it happened: once I came to visit Marina Petrovna, and—bang!—she turned bald. And that was that.

Translated from the Russian by Valzhyna Mort

With a Key That Keeps Changing

Paul Celan

With a key that keeps changing
you unlock the house—inside:
the snowdrifts of what's never spoken.
The key changes in keeping
with the blood that wells up
from eye or mouth or ear

If your key changes, the word changes,
allowed to drift with the snowflakes. Depending
on the wind that pushes you away,
the snow packs round your word.

Translated from the German by David Young

Act of Gratitude

Francesc Parcerisas

Thank you, angel. Thank you, demons of the night.
Thank you, winter where the heart burns
arid tree-trunks of desire. Thank you,
bracing cold light, nocturnal water.
Thank you, midnight bile,
laurel of morning, hoopoe of dawn.
For what's odd, unexpected, wild,
for evil and pain, thank you.
For the sum of what we are
and are not,
for all we avoid
and all we crave.
Thanks for the lush words,
love and silver,
for yourself and myself.
Thank you for yes and for no.
For the ability to give thanks
and for rendering them unnecessary.
Thanks for fear,
for bread and oil,
for the night time.
Thank you for lovemaking
at the break of day, for the coin
discovered on the ground,
for your hand on my cheek,
the gush of the fountain.
Thank you for your eyes and lips,

for crying out my name with joy.
Many thanks, death, for your existence,
for making all these things
more vivid inside me—so very yours,
so beautiful, brimming, and complete.

Translated from the Catalan by Cyrus Cassells

Destinies

Gzar Hantoosh

The retired man
The brown crane-like boy
The woman with the blue shawl
And the poet with the diamond heart
Are waiting for the red bus
That will take them.
The retired man to:
Café "Hasan Ajmi"
The brown crane-like boy
To the Boy Scout Center
The woman with the blue shawl:
To al-Mansoor
And the poet with the diamond heart
To Hell.

Translated from the Arabic by Saadi Simawe

I Corinthians 13:11

Jericho Brown

When I was a child, I spoke as a child.
I even had a child's disease. I ran
From the Doberman like all children
On my street, but old men called me
Special. The Doberman caught up,
Chewed my right knee. Limp now
In two places, I carried a child's Bible
Like a football under the arm that didn't
Ache. I was never alone. I owned
My brother's shame of me. I loved
The words *thou* and *thee*. Both meant
My tongue in front of my teeth.
Both meant a someone speaking to me.
So what if I itched. So what if I couldn't
Breathe. I climbed the cyclone fence
Like children on my street and went
First when old men asked for a boy
To pray or to read. Some had it worse—
Nobody whipped me with a water hose
Or a phone cord or a leash. Old men
Said I'd grow into my face, and I did
Before I died.

Wild Youth
Sigurdur Pálsson

Crumbling bread behind the sofa
Plucking the buds from the most optimistic flower
Cursing in church as much as you dare
Making garlands of swearwords in the meadow
Blocking the waterbutt
Darting after the chickens
Throwing rocks into the barn
Pissing on the dog

Then going inside and kissing mother, smiling

Translated from the Icelandic by Bernard Scudder

The Necklace

Osip Mandelstam

Take, from my palms, for joy, for ease,
A little honey, a little sun,
That we may obey Persephone's bees.

You can't untie a boat unmoored.
Fur-shod shadows can't be heard,
Nor terror, in this life, mastered.

Love, what's left for us, and of us, is this
Living remnant, loving revenant, brief kiss
Like a bee flying completed dying hiveless

To find in the forest's heart a home,
Night's neverending hum,
Thriving on meadowsweet, mint, and time.

Take, for all that is good, for all that is gone,
That it may lie rough and real against your collarbone,
This string of bees, that once turned honey into sun.

Translated from the Russian by Christian Wiman

Psalm II

Georg Trakl

Stillness. The kind the blind might find beside an autumn wall,
Eavesdropping with worn-out brows on an unkindness of ravens.
Autumn's golden stillness: the face of the father in the guttering
    sunlight.
In the evening, the old village recedes into a hush of brown oaks,
The red hammering of the blacksmith, the beating of a heart.
Stillness; under fluttering sunflowers, the handmaiden hides her
    hyacinth brow
In her slow hands. Fear and silence—
The twilit room fills with splintering eyes, the hesitant steps
Of the old women, the purpled mouth dissolving in the dark.

The evening, wine-quiet. From the ceiling's low beams
A night moth dropped, nymph entombed in bluish sleep.
In the courtyard, a farmhand slaughters a lamb, our brows clouded by
    the sweet smell
Of the blood, the dark coolness of the fountain.
Dying asters grieving over their own sad vanishings, that's what those
    windy-golden voices are.
When night falls, you gaze at me from failing eyes.
In blue stillness, your cheeks crumbled into dust.

A brushfire burns out so quietly. The black hamlet falls silent on its
    little plot of land,
As if the cross itself climbed down from the blue hill of Calvary.
The silent earth heaved up its dead.

Translated from the German by Jay Hopler

The Cradle Autumn 1901
Steve Scafidi

Kneeling down on the box, two plumbers cut a small
   square over where it was guessed the face looked out
and the lead lining—soft for tools—cut easy

in 1901 when his coffin was opened the last time
   and seventeen men peered in to verify it was him—
Abraham Lincoln—lying, so long dead inside.

They reported a yellow mold all over the black suit
   he had worn to his Second Inaugural. They reported
the small tuft of beard the coroner left prickly

on the president's chin after shaving his face in death.
   The flag buried with him was just dots and rags
and a smell shot up to gag the children and the one

curious dog who stood nearby. They reported his face,
   a light green from the funeral powder, had turned
to lay sideways on the satin pillow. They reported

to Robert that it was his father and closed the thing
   for good laying the box in a cage of steel onto which
was poured four hundred tons of concrete. However

it was not reported that the sun burned like a mansion
   in the November sky and that just before the workers
sealed the window one reached a fingertip in to touch

the mole above the dead man's lip. He said it felt like
   the shock he got as a boy in a storm he thought was over.
Electric, but colder. A bee sting, burning ice and smolder.

Flee
Katie Ford

When the transistor said *killing wind*
I felt myself a small noise

a call sign rubbed out
but still live where light
cut through the floorboards

and don't you think I dreamed the light a sign

didn't I want to cross
the water of green beads breaking
where one saw the other last

where the roof was torn
and the dome cried out
that the tearing was wide and far

and this is not just a lesson
of how to paint an X upon a house
how to mark one dead in the attic
two on the floor

didn't I wish
but didn't I flee

when the cries fell through
the surface of light
and the light stayed light
as if to say nothing or
what do you expect me to do

I am not human

I gave you each other
so save each other.

Whitethorn

Jacqueline Osherow

As always, when I see it, my first thought:
some kids' discarded tissues, helped by wind,
have scattered in the hedge, caught on thorns, not
look! winter's finally at an end
not *this is what it means to bloom for whitethorn.*
It's my greatest failing. I never learn
or, rather, don't apply the things I know,
which is why I have so little to show
for my quickly coming up on fifty years.
But who wants to know that spring is tatters
of dingy whiteness clinging to a briar?
Can't just one bush blaze with fire—
for a single instant—that does not consume?
Or is this my vision? this stingy bloom?

Supper
Youssef al-Sayigh

Every evening when I come home
my sadness comes out of his room
wearing his winter overcoat
and walks behind me.
I walk, he walks with me,
I sit, he sits next to me,
I cry, he cries for my cry,
until midnight
when we get tired.
At that point
I see my sadness goes into the kitchen
opens the refrigerator,
takes a black piece of meat
and prepares my supper.

Translated from the Arabic by Saadi Simawe

["The poet said to his soul ... "]

Lluís Roda

The poet said to his soul:
—I am tired of the weight of my feet on the ground;
I want to entwine and twist any two strati
And make them be one
And lower myself up, rappel good and high
To where you are, from where you souls are from,
From where I never left
And by this linen of white clouds knotted
Like an umbilical cord,
Allow myself to drop, disallow myself alone,
Break off my window's bars; break out of my conditions
Karmic or penal, disallow my torment,
This fear that imprisons, and I'm condemned
And I am locked in shadow
At all times sentried by insensible sorrow
Chained to high ramparts unreal and all mine,
The most massive and latent walls of my mind,
Intimate, dense and impregnable;
And in the damp corner in shackles, where
Life infiltrates, the rats are welcome
To be company in my loneliness
With their infectious messages
Of slime and putrefaction.
It is a lengthy and capital punishment
This sensing you and not finding you
This finding you and not sensing you.

Translated from the Catalan by Michael Odom

from Third Call and Other Rarities

Brenda Solís-Fong

Everything sometimes seems
a sport
in which I
cover myself with a finger
and squirm,
revolt,
light palaces on fire,
and cover my body
in spots.

*   *   *

My innocence is intact
except sometimes
my fingernails come out
sharp in self-defense.

Translated from the Spanish by Daagya Dick and Jesse Nathan

The Stonemason's Son Contemplates Death

Shadab Zeest Hashmi

Because my heart
became a kiln
I wished to die

The inscription on the tiles
made a prayer in butterfly script
crowning your well

May the water refresh your soul

The clanging of keys became loud
A soldier stood behind me pissing in the well

Someone sang in the distance
Couldn't tell if she was a Jew
Christian or Muslim

It was a devotional song

Three Poems
Vera Pavlova

A muse inspires when she comes.
A wife inspires when she leaves.
A mistress inspires when she does not come.
Shall I do all of that at one and the same time?

*   *   *

and there was light
in my belly
and I closed my eyes
not to blind you
and I covered my face
like Moses
and you saw
that for me
it was good

*   *   *

Last will is a plan of a life done with.
At my funeral I do not want to hear
Rakhmaninov's "Prelude in C minor,"
nor Beethoven's *allegretto* from the Seventh,
nor anything from my beloved Chaikovsky.
I want Mozart's "Piano Concerto in A major,"

Mahler's *adagietto* from the Fifth, and Bruckner's Ninth, third movement. But the choice is yours: weepers choose the music.

Translated from the Russian by Steven Seymour

Ways of Loving (IV)

Carmelia Leonte

Oh God, what a long time has passed from yesterday to now.
As if a mountain had collapsed
at the threshold of morning.
As if a plagued town set itself on fire
and we ceremoniously bear our bones through it.
You say you're my father?
If so, why do the silver forks of the orphanage
clang in my pocket?
Are you my bridegroom?
Then where's the tarnished gold of your vow?
I love you, you tell me.
I love you, I reply.
On our shoulders
predatory birds nest.

Translated from the Romanian by Mihaela Moscaliuc

Elegy for Kenneth Koch

Fred Moramarco

d. July 6, 2002

It seems too crazy, like one of your mad, funny poems,
that you're not with us any more, not here to point out
the *thisness* of things, like mountains, circuses, and fresh air.
You were always the court jester of poets,
toppling pretension from its granite and marble heights.
"Look," you would say, about this or that,
"how absolutely strange, marvelous, and ordinary it is,
like everything else you will meet on your daily rounds."
You noticed the blueness of blue, the curvature of the round,
the still beats of silence within seconds.
One of my favorites of your lines is
"To learn of cunnilingus at fifty
Argues a wasted life." This from your poem,
"Some General Instructions," which pings in my head even today.
Ah, Kenneth, the obit said it was leukemia and you were 77.
Hard to imagine either. You, a frail old man, eaten by blood cells.
I rarely saw you when you weren't laughing, darting here and there.
I remember we wrote a sestina in your class,
each student writing a line as the poem went around the room.
I wrote the last line of that poem, and remember it forty years later
because you thought it was the perfect ending:
"Who would have guessed at such a meaning for summer?"
And I say that again, for this summer, when you're no longer here:
Who would have guessed at such a meaning for summer?

The Game

Charles Baudelaire

Old ladies of the night, in faded chairs,
with eyebrows penciled on, and winning looks,
simpering and ogling, angling their small ears
till stone and metal dance with little clicks;

around green baize, faces with no lips,
lips with no color, jaws devoid of teeth,
infernally twitching, searching fingertips
groping through empty pockets, picking at cloth;

dusty chandeliers, a grubby room,
enormous oil lamps doling out dim light
to famous poets, foreheads wracked with gloom,
sitting round squandering their bloody sweat.

That's the black tableau that I was shown
once in a dream. Or was it second sight?—
I saw myself there watching in that den,
cold and mute and envious of their lot;

envious of the men's tenacious passion
and the dismal gaiety of those old whores
trafficking to my face some final ration
of the beauty and hauteur that once was theirs.

But how could I envy them? Poor folk who'll lose
all they are, yet run on with elation
towards the abyss, so drunk on life they'd choose
pain over death, hell over annihilation.

Translated from the French by Jan Owen

The Trap

Sandra Alcosser

For Christmas I gave him a jar
of three-fruit marmalade made
with barley water. He spooned it
after dinner, admiring the color
of pore and rind.

Once again we slept together
back to back, husband and wife.
All night I wanted to turn, open
my arms, but I remembered last summer
alone in the new place, how I watched
a mouse lick soft brie from a trap
I'd set. The spring was rusty. It took
a long time to snap.

The Big War
Charles Simic

We played war during the war,
Margaret. Toy soldiers were in big demand,
The kind made from clay.
The lead ones they melted into bullets, I suppose.

You never saw anything as beautiful
As those clay regiments! I used to lie on the floor
For hours staring them in the eye.
I remember them staring back at me in wonder.

How strange they must have felt
Standing stiffly at attention
Before a large, incomprehending creature
With a moustache made of milk.

In time they broke, or I broke them on purpose.
There was a wire inside their limbs,
Inside their chests, but nothing in the heads!
Margaret, I made sure.

Nothing at all in the heads ...
Just an arm, now and then, an officer's arm,
Wielding a saber from a crack
In my deaf grandmother's kitchen floor.

All Good Conductors

Christian Wiman

1.

O the screech and heat and hate
we have for each day's commute,

the long wait at the last stop
before we go screaming

underground, while the pigeons
court and shit and rut

insolently on the tracks
because this train is always late,

always aimed at only us,
who when it comes with its

blunt snout, its thousand mouths,
cram and curse and contort

into one creature, all claws and eyes,
tunneling, tunneling, tunneling

toward money ...

2.

Sometimes a beauty
cools through the doors at Grand,

glides all the untouchable
angles and planes

of herself
to stand among us

like a little skyscraper,
so sheer, so spare,

gazes going all over her
in a craving wincing way

like sun on glass ...

3.

There is a dreamer
all good conductors

know to look for
when the last stop is made

and the train is ticking cool,
some lover, loner, or fool

who has lived so hard
he jerks awake

in the graveyard,
where he sees

coming down the aisle
a beam of light

whose end he is,
and what he thinks are chains

becoming keys ...

Turtle
Youssef al-Sayigh

A turtle entered our house.
We were very disturbed.
My wife said:
—Throw it out.
Our neighbor said:
—Kill it.
The maid said ...
The Imam said ...
All the neighbors gathered
and every one suggested a solution
while the turtle was listening
while the turtle was weeping upon herself
and us.

Translated from the Arabic by Saadi Simawe and Chuck Miller

For the Woman with the Radio

Malena Mörling

Everywhere we are either moving away from
    or toward one another,
in cars, on buses or bicycles.

      We are either moving
or not moving. But yesterday in one
           of the interminable hallways of the hospital

I suddenly heard Bach
    and when I looked up
the music was arcing

      about the paralyzed, middle-aged body
of a woman rolling face first toward me
         on a bed with wheels.

The soprano was endlessly falling
    into the well
of her voice and we were on the earth

      and this was this life
when we would meet
         and depart there in the hall

where the hectic dust particles were mixing
    in the sunlight
in the air, between the green tiles on the walls.

curriculum vitae
Eugenius Ališanka

I was born hungry
graduated from the game of hopscotch
certified melancholic
all my life I've been a day laborer
most prestigious job—a pickpocket
briefly, I worked as an acolyte for one god
and then as a pine-box carpenter for another
at present I do seasonal work as a writer
I live alone with a wife and son
I've launched more books than I've written
issued dozens of requisitions
appeals and communiqués
several apologies
this year one to a traffic cop
received a prize from the ministry of culture
I am the laureate of the train marathon
I should request a job to match my specialty
something grounded earthy
maybe as a shepherd
with a fife for my salary

Translated from the Lithuanian by Kerry Shawn Keys and the author

Passage

Fady Joudah

I'm more exhausted than a crossroads
the horses I never rode
the magnetic fields filled with souls
of past riders and the horses' past souls

or the plastic horses I lined up
for my child-
hood windows

Soon thought will be found out
a necktie tenderness in treeless terrain

The dead proliferate like capital
or are a spawn
forgetfulness devours

I'm more exhausted than a crossroads
thought will be found a chromosome
and grief a brief allele

where victims and who isn't today
console me and say
your heart is still beating

you're still dying

100

Yu Jian

The afternoon sun
sweeps across the furniture deep into the room
lights up the bowls and plates in the cupboard
the salt and pepper shakers on the gas stove
and the square stool under the table
The sun rearranges the colors in the pantry
A flash in the darkness
I find the long-lost
silver spoon

Translated from the Chinese by Wang Ping and Ron Padgett

Strange Things
Don Share

    After Góngora

I have seen, my Celalba, strange things:
    split clouds, broken-mouthed winds,
high towers kissing their own foundations,
    and the earth expelling its guts;

bridges bending like tensile stems;
    prodigious streams, violent rivers,
bad crossings through great currents
    and worse bridlings in the mountains;

days like Noah's, fine people
    in the highest-rising pine trees,
in the greatest, most robust beech trees—

shepherds, dogs, cabins, and cattle,
    over the waters I saw them, formless, lifeless,
and nothing more than my own cares troubled me.

It Was August, It Was August
Carol Frost

and she was dancing, no, we three were dancing.
Her paranoia wasn't yet Thracian.
I thought of the greenhouse in Vienna,

my grandmother, her mother, dancing
while her partner's wife sat stone-lipped
among roses in the Viennese greenhouse.

I was young, what do the young know
of forgivable sin? I was stone-lipped.
My husband was singing, while dancing,

his sin his innocence—how old must one be to know
that sexual beauty is dangerous at any age?
My husband sang "Embraceable You" and danced,

mother dipped toward him, and he turned
to her. She'd want to tear him to pieces,
but she didn't know that

until in the end he spurned her—
her mind jangled like bees in a sac.
But she didn't know that.
It was August, it was only August.

My Wife's Spine
Jarosław Mikołajewski

And when my wife's pregnant
her spine is a bough
breaking under the weight of apples

humble all the way down to earth
from lack of resistance

On nights of keeping watch
her spine is a scarf
tightened around a slender neck

On nights of animal love
it is the zipper in a suitcase
that won't close, even under a knee

On nights of human love
it is the steel rope
rustling in the wind, at the highest voltage

On the noon walk
my wife's spine is the flag
carried by the pilgrims' guide in a crowded church

In the evening, reduced by the march,
her spine is a bunch of frightened kids
who broke the kindergarten's piano

it is the keyboard
of the broken piano

When she takes a shower
her spine is a viper
lazing watchfully on a sizzling road

Under the midnight comforter
my wife's spine is like a splinter burning in the oven
from which I'll pull out warm bread at dawn

Translated from the Polish by Piotr Florczyk

["All people are pregnant, said Diotima ... "]
Hasso Krull

All people are pregnant, said Diotima,
their bodies are pregnant, their souls are pregnant,
oh how they want to give birth with all their might.
Beauty is childbirth. Birth is beautiful.

So Diotima said to Socrates. Socrates said
the same thing at Agathon's party, and it was heard
by young Aristodemus, and he passed it on
to Apollodorus, who told his own friends.

Little Plato was playing with beetles in the garden.
Where did all these beetles come from, he wondered,
did they emerge suddenly from an immense, flawless beetle
in the sky? That we are unable to see?

At night, his mommy carried him inside and put him to sleep.
At Agathon's place a party of pederasts began,
and because no one could stand to drink any more they began to argue:
let us talk of love. Let us talk of beauty.

Translated from the Estonian by Brandon Lussier

from Flower World Variations: Song of a Dead Man
Yaqui

I do not want these flowers
    moving
        but the flowers
want to move
    I do not want these flowers
        moving
but the flowers
    want to move
        I do not want these flowers
moving
    but the flowers
        want to move
out in the flower world
    the dawn
        over a road of flowers
I do not want these flowers
    moving
        but the flowers
want to move
    I do not want these flowers
        moving
but the flowers
    the flowers
        want to move

English version by Jerome Rothenberg

Autumn
Leonardo Sinisgalli

The flies seem glad
to see me again.
They inch along the stems
of my glasses, pounce
on the tips of my ears.
The white paper fascinates them.
I talk, I pet them,
gather them in my fist,
call them by name,
Fantina, Filomena, Felicetta.
I fool myself thinking
it's always them.
One checks his reflection in my fingernail,
the others hide so that
he'll have to find them.

Translated from the Italian by W.S. Di Piero

Caynham Camp

G.C. Waldrep

1.

Through curtains, winter light. Late Mandelstam
open on the table. "Exile" means we are still in this life,
we are still in love with this life
where a fleet steams by in midnight Latin, new ghosts
for whom the heart crochets a new song. It's their birthday
and, like children, they know. Like children
they capture insects to pull off their wings,
tie threads to the fragile legs of honeybees and wasps.
It is cold where the children are, but so brightly lit.
I read Mandelstam in the morning. I am not abandoned.
At the supermarket it's all I can do
to point to the meat I want, pink jewel in its crystal case.

2.

I photographed the hollies by the in-turned gate,
something regal, or as if the hill had developed lips, as if
the summit were working slowly
back towards a capacity for speech. My own tongue
a debt in it, a stud. I had barely spoken to anyone
in weeks, nodding to the waiter
at the dim French restaurant as if I were a foreigner.
I took a wrong turn in the medieval quarter

and found myself part of a procession, dark-clad, silent.
It was an accident, I wanted to say,
only to remember that once again I'd been cast
in the thief's role, which is why from every
house we passed I recognized an ancient, accusing glare.

3.

The district opened on a grid of broken stone
punctuated by pasture; the larger mammals
shifted randomly, with the gentle Brownian motion
of hunger that has not yet reached despair, cannot imagine
that with some slight displacement of the body
every desire won't be met.
Then they were all around me, an encircling gravity.
I bowed, as only one fairly caught
in trespass may bow. I recognized the incised
language on the sentry trunks
and copied it carefully into the flesh of my eye
so that I could teach it to the offending light, which buzzed
drunkenly against my shins, my temples, my chest.

4.

And then, as if in some half-forgotten children's tale,
I found myself an inheritor
of a tiny kingdom, misted with marsh gas
and briar's rank exhaust, depleted of its saints.
The people who lived there used the wounds of red grapes
as their currency. I met a few of them;
they made a small living as pipefitters, and they professed

never to have heard of me, or where I lived.
They claimed that if you dug under the ground
you'd find no evidence at all of any prior human settlement.

5.

They trapped songbirds and sold them on the open market.
They gave nothing as alms. I liked a few of them,
mostly the women. Perhaps the problem
was that I did not, as I'd been taught, exit as I'd entered.
Now the season touches me
in a way that feels both more distant and less hindered,
days laundered not in war but in rumors
of war's creche, past and future. For days I slide letters
unopened across my kitchen table; when I finally
do open them I don't read them, merely leave them folded
like quiet hands in the matte lap of each torn envelope.

In the rose I waited for the sermon to break,
the last book close. I held a petal to the surface of my eye.

Autumn Day

Rainer Maria Rilke

Lord: it is time. The summer was immense.
Stretch out your shadow on the sundial's face,
and on the meadows let the winds go loose.

Command the last fruits to be full in time,
grant them even two more southerly days,
press them toward fulfillment soon, and chase
the last sweetness into the heavy wine.

Whoever has no house now, will build none.
Who is alone now, will stay long alone,
will lie awake, read, get long letters written,
and through the streets that follow up and down
will wander restless, when the leaves are driven.

Translated from the German by John Felstiner

Snow

Zhang Shuguang

Snow, I was surprised. The first snow
choked in my throat,
I wanted to cough, to run
from snow.
I didn't see the street, the poplars, the park benches
the conductor's whistle. Snow.
Faces of idiots abused the air
and turned to snow.
I didn't have a chance to read "The Massacre"
or "The Dead" by Joyce.
I didn't know death and snow
are colleagues.
I was three that year, Mother threw me up in the air, a tree in the yard.
Now we don't live in snow—
Mother's nostrils don't breathe. 1982.

Translated from the Chinese by Katie Farris with Ming Di

6th Floor

Bruno K. Öijer

you are no longer cold
you feel neither hunger nor thirst
you like your life
you never got lost on your travels

I lay here, heard you tiptoe
out during the nights, undress
the river and
place the water beside your body

Translated from the Swedish by Malena Mörling and Jonas Ellerström

Masses

César Vallejo

At the end of the battle
a soldier was dying.
A man approached
and said to him, "I love you, don't go!"
but the dead man went on dying.

Two more arrived, they echoed,
"Don't leave us! Courage! Come back to life!"
but the dead man went on dying.

Twenty came to him, a hundred, a thousand, half a million
clamoring, "So much love, yet powerless against death!"
and the dead man went on dying.

Millions of men surrounded him
with one please in common, "Stay brother!"
but the dead man went on dying.

Then all the men of the earth encircled him.
The dead man watched them, in misery, overwhelmed.
He rose up slowly,
embraced the first man, and began to walk.

Translated from the Spanish by H. Alluri, M. Benedetto, K. Cordero, and E. Larsen

Old Grief
Leonardo Sinisgalli

The old cry easily.
In broad daylight,
sitting in a secret part of the empty house,
they burst into tears,
surprised by infinite despair.
They lift a sliver of pear
to their parched lips, the flesh
of a fig sun-baked on roof tiles.
Even a sip of water
can cool a crisis,
even this visit by a snail.

Translated from the Italian by B.H. Boston

Keeping Still
Pablo Neruda

Now we will count to twelve
and let's keep quiet.

For once on earth
let's not talk in any language;
let's stop for one second,
and not move our arms so much.

A moment like that would smell sweet,
no hurry, no engines,
all of us at the same time
in need of rest.

Fishermen in the cold sea
would stop harming whales
and the gatherer of salt
would look at his hurt hands.

Those who prepare green wars,
wars with gas, wars with fire,
victories with no survivors,
would put on clean clothes
and go for a walk with their brothers
out in the shade, doing nothing.

Just don't confuse what I want
with total inaction;

it's life and life only;
I'm not talking about death.

If we weren't so single-minded
about keeping our lives moving
and could maybe do nothing for once,
a huge silence might interrupt this sadness
of never understanding ourselves,
of threatening ourselves with death;
perhaps the earth could teach us;
everything would seem dead
and then be alive.

Now I will count up to twelve
and you keep quiet
and I will go.

Translated from the Spanish by Dan Bellm

Constantin Acosmei
Tirgu Neamt, Romania
A Romanian poet whose collection
*Jucaria mortului (The Dead Man's
Toy)* has been published in four
subsequently enlarged editions,
Constantin Acosmei holds a BA and
an MA in Romanian and French
Literatures from the University of
Iasi. His work can also be found in
Of Gentle Wolves (2011), an anthol-
ogy of Romanian poetry edited by
Martin Woodside. Acosmei lives a
quiet withdrawn life in Iasi with his
beautiful wife Lia.

Zubair Ahmed
Dhaka, Bangladesh
Zubair Ahmed's first full-length
collection of poetry, *City of Rivers*,
was published in 2012 by McSwee-
ney's. Ahmed grew up in Dhaka,
Bangladesh, and immigrated to
the U.S. with his family after they
won the Diversity Visa Lottery. He
graduated from Stanford University
in 2013 with an MS in mechanical
engineering.

Youssef al-Sayigh (1930–2005)
Mosul, Iraq
Youssef al-Sayigh has authored several
poetry collections, including *Confes-
sions of Malik bin al-Rayib, Vol. I and II*
(1972). An active member of the Iraqi
Communist Party, al-Sayigh faced
imprisonment and, following his sen-
tencing, voiced support for the Ba'ath
Party under the threat of exile.

Sandra Alcosser
Washington, D.C., U.S.
Sandra Alcosser was the first
"Conservation Poet" for both the
Wildlife Conservation Society and
Poets House, and Montana's first poet
laureate. Her 1998 collection, *Except
by Nature*, won the James Laughlin
Award. Alcosser founded San Diego
State University's MFA program,
where she currently teaches poetry,
fiction, and feminist poetics.

Eugenijus Ališanka
Barnaul, Soviet Union
Eugenijus Ališanka has served as edi-
tor for the Lithuanian *Vilnius Review*
since 2003. Having studied math-
ematics at Vilnius University and
later serving in the military, Ališanka
has authored five poetry collections
and two books of essays. Ališanka
is considered one of contemporary
Lithuania's most important poets.

Rae Armantrout
Vallejo, Calif., U.S.
Rae Armantrout is a professor of
poetry and poetics, and the director
of the New Writing Series at the Uni-
versity of California, San Diego. Her
Collected Prose was published in 2007,
and she received the 2010 Pulitzer
Prize for Poetry for *Versed*.

Charles Baudelaire (1821–1867)
Paris, France
Charles Baudelaire is considered one
of the most influential poets of the

nineteenth century. His best-known collection of poems—his debut *Les Fleurs du mal* (*The Flowers of Evil*)—was published in 1857. Baudelaire faced criticism for the "profane" nature of the book, though it remained highly acclaimed, then as now.

Ana Blandiana
Timișoara, Romania
Ana Blandiana is president of the Romanian PEN Club and founder and president of the Civic Alliance, work for which she received the Légion d'Honneur (2009). In 1993, Blandiana created the Memorial for the Victims of Communism and of the Resistance. Her collection *My Native Land A4* was published in English in 2010.

Eavan Boland
Dublin, Ireland
The daughter of a diplomat and a painter, Eavan Boland is one of the most beloved living poets of Ireland. She directs the Creative Writing Program at Stanford University, where she has taught since 1995.

Yves Bonnefoy (1923–2016)
Tours, France
In addition to poetry, Bonnefoy was renowned for his art criticism and translations of Shakespeare. In 1980, when Bonnefoy inherited Roland Barthes's position as chair of comparative poetics at the Collège de France, he became the first poet to join the institution since Valéry, in 1937.

Geoffrey Brock
Atlanta, Ga., U.S.
Geoffrey Brock received an MFA from the University of Florida and a PhD from the University of Pennsylvania. Brock won a Guggenheim Fellowship in support of his 2012 anthology, *The FSG Book of 20th-Century Italian Poetry*. Brock's poem "Star Frago Mashup" incorporates language from Frago 242, published by Wikileaks in 2010 as part of the Iraq War Logs.

Jericho Brown
Shreveport, La., U.S.
An associate professor of English and creative writing at Emory University, Jericho Brown earned a PhD from the University of Houston and an MFA from the University of New Orleans. His two books, *Please* (2008) and *The New Testament* (2014), have received widespread acclaim, the former winning the American Book Award.

Peter Campion
Boston, Mass., U.S.
Poet and art critic Peter Campion has authored three collections of poetry: *Other People* (2005), *The Lions* (2009), and *El Dorado* (2013). Recipient of the 2010 Joseph Brodsky Rome Prize from the American Academy of Arts and Letters, Campion directs the Creative Writing Program at the University of Minnesota.

Paul Celan (1920–1970)
Chernivtsi, Ukraine (Czernovitz, Romania)
While Celan lost both his parents
to a concentration camp during
World War II, he was able to escape,
ultimately travelling to Paris. Fluent
in Russian, French, and Romanian,
Celan made his living as a translator.
Celan received both the Bremen Prize
for German Literature and the Georg
Buchner Prize.

Victoria Chang
Detroit, Mich., U.S.
Victoria Chang's fourth book of poems
is *Barbie Chang* (2017). Her previous
book, *The Boss* (2013), won the PEN
Center USA Literary Award and a
California Book Award. She received
a Guggenheim Fellowship in 2017.
Chang lives in Southern California and
teaches at Chapman University and
Orange County School of the Arts.

Xi Chuan
Xuzhou, China
One of contemporary China's most
prominent poets, Xi Chuan has
published five collections of poetry.
He has taught at the University of
Iowa, New York University, and the
Central Academy of Fine Arts in
Beijing. Chuan's many awards include
the Modern Chinese Poetry Prize and
the Lu Xun Prize.

Mahmoud Darwish (1941–2008)
Al-Birweh, Palestine
Mahmoud Darwish and his family

fled to Lebanon when he was seven to
escape the Israeli Army. Darwish's work
is preoccupied with alienation and the
pluralism of Arabic identity. His oeuvre
includes more than thirty collections
of poetry and eight books of prose.

Kwame Dawes
Accra, Ghana
Although born in Ghana, Kwame
Dawes spent much of his childhood
in Jamaica—a source of inspiration
for his seventeen collections of
poetry. An actor, playwright, essayist,
novelist, and singer, Dawes is also
the recipient of an Emmy for the
interactive website HOPE: Living and
Loving with HIV in Jamaica.

Carol Ann Duffy
Glasgow, Scotland
Scottish poet and playwright Carol
Ann Duffy was the first female Scot-
tish poet laureate in its four-century
history. She studied philosophy at
the University of Liverpool, and is
renowned for her multidisciplinary
poetic performances.

Michael Dumanis
Moscow, Russia
Michael Dumanis received a BA from
Johns Hopkins University, an MFA
from the Iowa Writers' Workshop,
and a PhD from the University of
Houston. *My Soviet Union*, Dumanis's
first collection, won the 2006 Juniper
Prize for Poetry, and that same year
he co-edited the anthology *Legitimate*

Dangers: American Poets of the New Century (2006).

Israel Emiot (1909–1978)
Ostrów Mazowiecka, Poland
Israel Emiot is known as one of the great Yiddish poets of the twentieth century. He survived World War II, prison, and exile. Emiot eventually settled in the United States.

Carolyn Forché
Detroit, Mich., U.S.
Poet, teacher, and activist Carolyn Forché often works at the intersection of the personal and the political. Her collections often confront acts of atrocious violence. In 1993, she published *Against Forgetting: Twentieth-Century Poetry of Witness*, which has become a landmark anthology.

Katie Ford
Portland, Ore., U.S.
Katie Ford studied theology and poetry at Harvard University and received an MFA from the Iowa Writers' Workshop. She is the author of *Deposition* (2002), *Colosseum* (2008), and *Blood Lyrics* (2014). Ford's work has appeared in *The New Yorker, Poetry, The Paris Review, The American Poetry Review*, and *Ploughshares*.

Tua Forsström
Porvoo, Finland
Tua Forsström is a Finnish author who writes in Swedish. She was awarded the Nordic Council's Literature Prize in 1998.

Carol Frost
Lowell, Mass., U.S.
Carol Frost studied at the Sorbonne, the State University of Oneonta, and Syracuse University, and her poetry collections include *Entwined: Three Lyric Sequences* (2014), *Honeycomb: Poems* (2010), and *Love and Scorn: New and Selected Poems* (2000).

Gloria Fuertes (1917–1998)
Madrid, Spain
A member of the first generation of post–Civil War poets in Spain, Fuertes published fifteen books of poetry and thirty-four children's books. Fuertes learned to read and write at the age of three, and in her sixties starred as a storyteller on a children's television program.

Rachel Galvin
Rochester, N.Y., U.S.
Poet and translator Rachel Galvin received a PhD in Comparative Literature from Princeton University, and is currently an assistant professor at the University of Chicago. Galvin's recent collection *Lost Property Unit* was a finalist for the 2011 National Poetry Series and the 2011 Kinereth Gensler Award.

Forrest Gander
Barstow, Calif., U.S.
Forrest Gander's most recent books are the translations *Alice Iris Red Horse: Poems by Yoshimasu Gozo* (2016) and *Then Come Back: The Lost Neruda Poems*

(2016). He grew up in Virginia and among other things studied geology in college.

David Gewanter
New York City, N.Y., U.S.
Poet, editor, and essayist David Gewanter has received a Whiting Writers' Award and a Witter Bynner Fellowship from the Library of Congress. He holds a PhD from the University of California, Berkeley, has published several collections of poetry, and co-edited the *Collected Poems of Robert Lowell* (2003).

John Glenday
Broughty Ferry, Scotland, UK
John Glenday is the author of four collections: *The Apple Ghost* (1989), winner of the Scottish Arts Council Book Award; *Undark* (1995); *Grain* (2009); and *The Golden Mean* (2015). Glenday studied English at the University of Edinburgh and worked as a psychiatric nurse following graduation.

Jacek Gutorow
Grodków, Poland
Polish poet Jacek Gutorow received a PhD from the University of Silesia in 1999. After completing his studies, he began working at the Institute of English Studies at the University of Opole. Gutorow's recognition includes a nomination for the Nike Literary Award and the Gdynia Literary Prize.

Rachel Hadas
New York City, N.Y., U.S.
Rachel Hadas studied classics at Harvard, poetry at Johns Hopkins, and comparative literature at Princeton, and has taught at Princeton University and Columbia University. Since 1981, she has taught at Rutgers University. She's the author of numerous collections of poetry and translation.

Gzar Hantoosh (c. 1945–2006)
Al-Diwaniyah, Iraq
Gzar Hantoosh began publishing poetry in the 1970s. His books include *The Red Forest* (1988) and *The Happiest Man in the World* (2001). Hantoosh studied engineering in Baghdad, and later worked in the Department of Agriculture and Agrarian Reform in Diwaniyah.

Shadab Zeest Hashmi
Lahore, Pakistan
Author of *Kohl & Chalk* (2013) and *Baker of Tarifa* (2010), Pakistani poet Shadab Zeest Hashmi has won the Nâzım Hikmet Poetry Prize and the San Diego Book Award. She also serves as Pakistan's representative on the website UniVerse: A United Nations of Poetry.

Seamus Heaney (1939–2013)
Castledawson, County Derry, Northern Ireland
Considered one of Ireland's most important poets, Seamus Heaney grew up as a Catholic in Protestant

Northern Ireland. His accolades include the the 2006 T.S. Eliot Prize and the 1995 Nobel Prize in Literature. Heaney's epitaph reads, WALK ON AIR AGAINST YOUR BETTER JUDGEMENT.

Nâzim Hikmet (1902–1963)
Thessaloniki, Greece
From 1928 to 1938, Nâzim Hikmet published nine books of poetry in Turkey. He left the country in 1951 following a jail sentence for "radical" political activity. Hikmet has been widely translated, and is often considered the first modern Turkish poet.

Edward Hirsch
Chicago, Ill., U.S.
Edward Hirsch is president of the John Simon Guggenheim Memorial Foundation and a chancellor of the Academy of American Poets. Hirsch's awards include a MacArthur Fellowship, a Guggenheim Fellowship, a Pablo Neruda Presidential Medal of Honor, and an Academy of Arts and Letters Award.

Jane Hirshfield
New York City, N.Y., U.S.
Poet, translator, and essayist Jane Hirshfield has authored eight books of poetry and two collections of essays. She took a nearly eight-year hiatus from writing to study at the San Francisco Zen Center. In 2004, Hirshfield received the Academy Fellowship from the Academy of American Poets.

Ishion Hutchinson
Port Antonio, Jamaica
Ishion Hutchinson's work has received international acclaim and has been translated into German, Polish, Russian, and Spanish. His first collection, *Far District: Poems* (2010), won the PEN/Joyce Osterweil Award. Hutchinson is the Meringoff Sesquicentennial Fellow Assistant Professor of English at Cornell University.

Ani Ilkov
Ruzhintsi, Bulgaria
Ani Ilkov co-founded the weekly publication *Literaturen Vestnik*, and has authored ten volumes of poetry—most recently, *Collected* (2011). He has taught at universities in India and Great Britain, and currently resides in Sofia.

Mark Irwin
Faribault, Minn., U.S.
Mark Irwin received an MFA from the Iowa Writers' Workshop and a PhD in English/comparative literature from Case Western Reserve University. Irwin has published seven poetry collections, most recently *American Urn: New & Selected Poems (1987–2011)*.

Yu Jian
Yunnan Province, China
During the Cultural Revolution, Jian's education was interrupted and his parents were forced into "re-education." Jian began experimenting with free

verse at age twenty, and started work on his long poem "Flight" in 1996. The final version, published in 2000, contains ten thousand Chinese characters and has been widely studied.

Fady Joudah
Austin, Texas, U.S.
The son of Palestinian refugees, Fady Joudah is a physician, poet, and translator. His first collection, *The Earth in the Attic*, won the 2007 Yale Series of Younger Poets competition. Joudah translated Mahmoud Darwish's final three collections of poetry, receiving the Banipal Prize.

Roberto Juarroz (1925–1995)
Coronel Dorrego, Argentina
Roberto Juarroz was an Argentine poet famous for his "poesia vertical," praised by the likes of Octavio Paz and Julio Cortázar.

Daniil Kharms (1905–1942)
Saint Petersburg, Russia
Soviet-era writer Daniil Kharms's work most often appeared in the children's magazines *Ezh* (*Hedgehog*) and *Chizh* (*Siskin*). He was arrested in 1931 for communicating anti-Soviet ideas through this children's literature, and later faced a series of imprisonments, arrests, and threats. In 1942, during the German blockade, Kharms died of hunger.

Yusef Komunyakaa
Bogalusa, La., U.S.
Yusef Komunyakaa served in the Vietnam War as a correspondent, and received a Bronze Star for his work as managing editor of *Southern Cross*, a military magazine. In 1994, Komunyakaa published *Neon Vernacular: New & Selected Poems 1977-1989*, which was awarded the Pulitzer Prize and the Kingsley Tufts Poetry Award.

Hasso Krull
Tallinn, Estonia
Hasso Krull is the author of several collections of poetry, including *Meeter and Demeeter* (2004), *Talv* (2006), and *Neli korda neli* (2009). His work is often concerned with mythologies and the Estonian landscape, and has been translated into Finnish, Swedish, English, French, German, Spanish, and Russian.

Carmelia Leonte
Botoşani, Romania
Carmelia Leonte is the author of four volumes of poetry, including *Graţia Viespilor* (*The Gracefulness of Wasps*, 2009), which was awarded the Writers' Union Prize. She has also published a novel, a children's book, translations from the work of Marguerite Duras, and numerous essays. Her first full-length collection in English, *The Hiss of the Viper* (translated by Mihaela Moscaliuc) was published by Carnegie Mellon University Press in 2015. She lives in Iasi, in northern Romania, where she works as an editor for the Museums Press.

Yan Li
Beijing, China

Chinese poet, novelist, and painter Yan Li's work has been translated into French, English, Italian, Swedish, Korean, and German. Following his move to the U.S., Li participated in the International Writing Program at the University of Iowa.

Federico García Lorca (1898–1936)
Fuente Vaqueros, Spain

Numbered among Spain's most esteemed poets and dramatists, Lorca published his first book, *Impresiones y Viajes* in 1919, but *Romancero gitano* (The Gypsy Ballads), published in 1928, was likely his most famous work. As a member of the artist group Generación del 27, Lorca became involved in the Spanish avant-garde alongside Salvador Dalí and Luis Buñuel.

Antonio Machado (1875–1939)
Seville, Spain

Poet and playwright Antonio Machado was born in Seville, Spain in 1875. After receiving his doctorate he moved to France, where he encountered the writers Jean Moréas and Oscar Wilde. Machado's early work was often linked to Romanticism, and his later work gestures towards landscape, solitude, and existentialism.

Nikola Madžirov
Strumica, Macedonia

Born to a family of Balkan war refugees, Nikola Madžirov's work often examines notions of escape and cultural identity. Madžirov has received the Studentski Zbor award, the Hubert Burda European Poetry Award, and a University of Iowa International Writing Residency.

Osip Mandelstam (1891–1938)
Warsaw, Poland

Osip Mandelstam's poetry was considered humanist and intuitive, departing from the symbolism of Russian poetry of the time. In 1933, Mandelstam wrote a poem disparaging Stalin and was arrested, tortured, and exiled. In 1938, following another arrest, the government reported that Mandelstam had died of heart failure.

Eric McHenry
Topeka, Kans., U.S.

Poet Laureate of Kansas, Eric McHenry is the author of several collections, and has been published in *The New Republic*, *Yale Review*, *The Guardian*, and *Poetry Daily*. He lives in Lawrence, Kansas, and teaches creative writing at Washburn University.

Dunya Mikhail
Baghdad, Iraq

Iraqi-American poet Dunya Mikhail was placed on Saddam Hussein's enemies list after working as a translator and journalist for the *Baghdad Observer*. She is the recipient of an Arab American Book Award and the United Nations Human Rights Award for

Freedom of Writing. In the mid-1990s, Mikhail immigrated to the U.S.

Jarosław Mikołajewski
Warsaw, Poland
Jarosław Mikołajewski is a Polish poet, writer, and translator. He is also the author of several children's books. The English translations of his works have appeared in *World Literature Today* and elsewhere.

Fred Moramarco (1938–2012)
Brooklyn, N.Y., U.S.
Founding Editor of *Poetry International*, Fred Moramarco was also a respected poet, literary critic, producer, director, and actor. In 2006, he co-produced *Hannah and Martin*, an award-winning show presented at the Lyceum Theater. Moramarco served as a professor of literature at San Diego State University.

Malena Mörling
Stockholm, Sweden
Malena Mörling has published two collections of poetry, *Ocean Avenue* (1999), winner of the New Issues Press Poetry Prize, and *Astoria* (2006). The recipient of a John Simon Guggenheim Foundation Fellowship, she currently lives in Santa Fe, New Mexico.

Valzhyna Mort
Minsk, Belarus
In 2005, Valzhyna Mort moved to the U.S. and published her first book, *I'm as Thin as Your Eyelashes*. In addition to authoring three poetry collections, Mort has edited two anthologies. Her most recent book, *Collected Body* (2011), is her first collection of poems composed entirely in English.

Pablo Neruda (1904–1973)
Parral, Chile
Beloved poet, political activist, and Nobel Laureate Pablo Neruda's work is often filled with eroticism and sensuous expressions of love. He was a committed communist, and published extensive works outlining his political ideas.

Bruno K. Öijer
Linköping, Sweden
Bruno K. Öijer was born in 1951 and is one of Sweden's most distinct and accomplished contemporary poets. He published his first collection of poems, *Song for Anarchism*, in 1973 and has since then published ten books of poetry, including his renowned *Trilogy* (2002) and most recently the collection, *And the Night Whispered Annabel Lee* in 2014. He is a tremendously popular performer of his work and draws huge crowds to his performances.

Jacqueline Osherow
Philadelphia, Pa., U.S.
Jacqueline Osherow's poetry has been anthologized in *Twentieth-Century American Poetry* (2003), *Jewish American Literature: A Norton Anthology* (2000), and *The Penguin Book of the Sonnet* (2001). She is a recipient of fellowships

from the Guggenheim Foundation and the NEA.

Kathleen Ossip
Albany, N.Y., U.S.
Professor at the New School in New York, Kathleen Ossip's most recent collection is *The Do-Over* (2015). Ossip's work has appeared in the *Washington Post, Best American Poetry, The Paris Review, Poetry,* and *The Believer.* She is a founding editor of the poetry review website *SCOUT.*

Alicia Ostriker
Brooklyn, N.Y., U.S.
Alicia Ostriker's work often explores Jewish identity and women's relationship to literature. She has been a finalist for the National Book Award twice, received a Guggenheim Fellowship, and won the Paterson Award, the San Francisco State Poetry Center Award, and the William Carlos Williams Award. Ostriker is a professor emerita of English at Rutgers University.

Sigurdur Pálsson
Skinnastadur, Iceland
Sigurdur Pálsson is an Icelandic poet who is also known as an author of children's books and as a translator. He also writes for theater and television.

Pandora
Pathein, Myanmar
The editor of *Tuning: An Anthology of Burmese Women Poets,* Pandora is a poet, essayist, and short story writer. She graduated from the University of Iowa's International Writing Program in 2012, and currently resides in Yangon.

Francesc Parcerisas
Begues, Spain
Considered a leading Catalan poet and translator of his generation, Francesc Parcerisas has published fourteen volumes of poetry. Parcerisas's awards include the 1966 Carles Riba Prize, the 1983 Critics' Prize for Catalan Poetry, and the 1983 Catalan Government Prize for Catalan Literature.

Vera Pavlova
Moscow, Russia
Russian poet Vera Pavlova began writing poetry at the age of twenty, in a maternity ward, following the birth of her first daughter. Since then, she has published fifteen collections of poetry in Russian, and her work has also appeared in American publications such as *Verse, Tin House,* and *The New Yorker.*

Francis Ponge (1899–1988)
Montpellier, France
One of France's most esteemed mid-century poets, Francis Ponge's prose poetry explores the character of everyday objects—a pebble, a cigarette, a bar of soap—and their capacity for complex appraisal. In 1974, Ponge became the third recipient of

the Neustadt International Prize for Literature.

Jacques Prévert (1900–1977)
Neuilly-sur-Seine, France
Poet and screenwriter Jacques Prévert is often associated with the Surrealist and Symbolist movements, though he also became engaged with a group of politically militant dramatists. He is perhaps best-known for his film scripts, including *Drôle de drame* (1937), *Les Visiteurs du soir* (1942), and *Les Enfants du paradis* (1944).

Mansur Rajih
Ta'iz Province, Yemen
A revolutionary poet and political activist, Mansur Rajih was imprisoned and sentenced to death on false charges of murder in 1983. His poems were smuggled from prison and printed in newspapers all over the Arab world. He was freed in 1998 following campaigns by Amnesty International and PEN International, and now lives in Norway.

Adrienne Rich (1929–2012)
Baltimore, Md., U.S.
Identifying as a lesbian Jew, poet and essayist Adrienne Rich inhabited a marginalized space and often interrogated the intricacies of that positioning in her work. Rich received many awards, including a MacArthur Foundation "genius grant" and a National Book Award for poetry. In 1997, she declined the National Medal of Arts.

Susan Rich
Brookline, Mass., U.S.
Author of four collections of poetry, Susan Rich studied at the University of Massachusetts, Harvard University, and the University of Oregon. Her collection *The Cartographer's Tongue* (2000) received the PEN U.S.A. Award for Poetry and the Peace Corps Writers Award.

Atsuro Riley
Charleston, S.C., U.S.
Atsuro Riley is the author of *Romey's Order* (University of Chicago Press, 2010), winner of the Kate Tufts Discovery Award, the Whiting Writers' Award, *The Believer* Poetry Award, and the Witter Bynner Award from the Library of Congress. Brought up in the South Carolina lowcountry, Riley lives in San Francisco.

Rainer Maria Rilke (1875–1926)
Prague, Czech Republic
One of the most beloved and lyrical twentieth-century poets, Rainer Maria Rilke's aesthetic was grounded in a complete embrace of life and experience, celebrating that which is often perceived as negative. Among his groundbreaking works are *Duineser Elegen* (*Duino Elegies*, 1923) and *Die Sonette an Orpheus* (*Sonnets to Orpheus*, 1923).

Yannis Ritsos (1909–1990)
Monemvasia, Greece
Yannis Ritsos's early life was riddled with hardship, including a stay at an

Athens sanatorium for tuberculosis, after which he developed an active interest in poetry and communism. A prolific poet, Ritsos was nominated for the Nobel Prize twice, and received the Lenin Peace Prize—the former Soviet Union's highest literary honor.

Lluís Roda
València, Spain

Lluís Roda is a poet, novelist, literary critic, philosopher, and translator. He became the "Poet of the City" of Barcelona after winning the Premi Jocs Florals de Barcelona in 2010, the highest poetry prize in Catalonia, for his poetry collection *Nadir*. Recent collections have won numerous additional awards.

Kay Ryan
San Jose, Calif., U.S.

Kay Ryan's 2010 collection, *The Best of It: New and Selected Poems*, received the Pulitzer Prize for Poetry. Ryan was appointed the U.S. Poet Laureate in 2008, and advocated strongly for community colleges during her two terms, having worked at a California community college for more than thirty years.

Tomaž Šalamun (1941–2014)
Zagreb, Croatia

Considered a leading voice of the Eastern European avant-garde, Tomaž Šalamun authored more than forty collections of poetry in Slovenian and English. Šalamun's first collection, *Poker* (1966), drew comparisons to poets such as Frank O'Hara, John Ashbery, and Charles Baudelaire. He went on to receive the Jenko Prize, and Slovenia's Prešeren and Mladost Prizes.

Steve Scafidi
Fairfax, Va., U.S.

Recipient of the Larry Levis Reading Prize, the James Boatwright Prize, and the Miller Williams Prize, Steve Scafidi lives in Summit Point, West Virginia, and works as a cabinetmaker. He has published several collections of poetry, including *Sparks from a Nine-Pound Hammer* (2001) and *For Love of Common Words* (2006).

Don Share
Cleveland, Ohio, U.S.

Editor of *Poetry* magazine since 2013, poet and translator Don Share has published three books of poetry, edited *Bunting's Persia* (2012), and co-edited *The Open Door: 100 Poems, 100 Years of Poetry Magazine* (2012). Share has won the *Times Literary Supplement* Translation Prize, the PEN/New England "Discovery" Award, and the Premio Valle Inclán.

Zhang Shuguang
Heilongjiang Province, China

Zhang Shuguang lives in Heilongjiang, in the northeast corner of China, but has been known nationwide since the early 1990s. He has translated Dante and Milosz (from English), and won the grand prize of the Poetry Construction Award in China in 2014.

Eleni Sikélianòs
Santa Barbara, Calif., U.S.
Eleni Sikélianòs has authored six collections of poetry, and has received a National Endowment for the Arts Fellowship, a Fulbright Fellowship, residencies at Princeton University, two Gertrude Stein Awards for Innovative American Writing, and the New York Council for the Arts Translation Award.

Charles Simic
Belgrade, Serbia
One of the most celebrated contemporary American poets, Charles Simic has received the Pulitzer Prize and served as the Poet Laureate of the United States. He immigrated to the U.S. when he was sixteen, in 1954. Simic has lived for many years on the shore of Bow Lake, in Strafford, New Hampshire.

Tracy K. Smith
Falmouth, Mass., U.S.
Tracy K. Smith is the author of three volumes of poetry: *Life on Mars* (2011), winner of the 2012 Pulitzer Prize for Poetry, *Duende* (2007), and *The Body's Question* (2003). From 1997-1999, she held a Stegner Fellowship at Stanford University. Smith currently teaches creative writing at Princeton University.

Leonardo Sinisgalli (1908–1981)
Montemurro, Italy
Leonardo Sinisgalli was an Italian poet and art critic, and author of numerous books. He studied engineering and mathematics, and later worked as an architect and a graphic designer. Sinisgalli founded the magazine *Civiltà delle Macchine*.

Ikkyū Sōjun (1394–1481)
Kyoto, Japan
Ikkyū Sōjun was an eccentric, iconoclastic Zen Buddhist monk and poet. He had a great impact on the infusion of Japanese art and literature with Zen attitudes and ideals.

Brenda Solís-Fong
San Jacinto, Guatemala
Brenda Solís-Fong's books of poetry include *Maquillando mis Alas* (2001) and *De Zancudos* (2001). The latter won the Guatemalan National Poetry Contest in 2001. She has done human rights work, and holds a degree in sociology from the University of San Carlos.

Marin Sorescu (1936–1996)
Bulzesti, Romania
Marin Sorescu's books include *Selected Poems* (1983), *The Biggest Egg in the World* (1987), and *Censored Poems* (2001). He often couched his political critique in tones of wit and mockery, and was eventually named Romania's Minister of Culture.

J. Hope Stein
Queens, N.Y., U.S.
J. Hope Stein is the author of the chapbooks *[Talking Doll]*: (2012) and *[Mary]*: (2012), and editor of poetrycrush.com.

Avrom Sutzkever (1913–2010)
Smorgon, Belarus
Yiddish poet Avrom Sutzkever was proclaimed "the greatest poet of the Holocaust" by *The New York Times* in 1984, and his body of work remains influential. Much of Sutzkever's early poetry was composed in Hebrew, and in 1985, he was awarded the Israel Prize for Yiddish literature.

Anna Swir (1909–1984)
Warsaw, Poland
Poet, playwright, and storyteller Anna Swir joined the Polish Resistance during World War II and worked as a military nurse during the Warsaw Uprising, narrowly avoiding execution. Her work has been translated into English in volumes such as *Happy as a Dog's Tail* (1985) and *Fat Like the Sun* (1986).

James Tate (1943–2015)
Kansas City, Mo., U.S.
James Tate's first collection, *The Lost Pilot* (1967), was selected for the Yale Series of Younger Poets when he was twenty-three. Tate authored more than twenty collections of poetry and received the National Book Award, a Pulitzer Prize, and the William Carlos Williams Award.

Georg Trakl (1887–1914)
Salzburg, Austria
Georg Trakl is considered one of the most important German poets of the early twentieth century. Trakl studied pharmaceutics at the University of Vienna, was drafted into the Austrian army under the medical corps, and later reenlisted after struggling to adjust to civilian life.

Tomas Tranströmer (1931–2015)
Stockholm, Sweden
Tomas Tranströmer's body of work was accompanied by the Lifetime Recognition Award from the Griffin Trust for Excellence in Poetry, the Swedish Academy's Nordic Prize, and a 2011 Nobel Prize in Literature. Tranströmer studied psychology and poetry at the University of Stockholm, and worked as a psychologist focused on youth in the prison system.

Marina Tsvetaeva (1892–1941)
Moscow, Russia
Numbered among the renowned poets of twentieth-century Russia, Marina Tsvetaeva published her first poetry collection, *Evening Album*, at the age of eighteen. During her lifetime, Russia experienced great turmoil, and she often lived in poverty.

Tristan Tzara (1896–1963)
Moineşti, Romania
Born to a wealthy Jewish family in Romania, Tristan Tzara eventually

moved to Zurich, where he became involved in the Dada movement. He was a communist sympathizer and member of the Resistance during the German occupation of Paris.

Jean Valentine
Chicago, Ill., U.S.
In 2015, Jean Valentine published her thirteenth book of poetry, *Shirt in Heaven*. Forty years earlier, she received the Yale Younger Poets Award for her first book, *Dream Barker*. Valentine earned her BA from Radcliffe College, and has taught at a number of institutions. She lives in New York City.

César Vallejo (1892–1938)
Santiago de Chuco, Peru
Born in a small town in the Andes, Vallejo published his first book of poems, *Los heraldos negros*, in 1919 to critical acclaim. It was followed, in 1922, with *Trilce*, in which, some critics have said, the poet invented surrealism before the Surrealists. He died in Paris.

Alissa Valles
Amsterdam, The Netherlands
Alissa Valles was born in Amsterdam to a Dutch mother and an American father. Her debut poetry collection, *Orphan Fire*, was published in 2008. Valles is a recipient of the Ruth Lilly Poetry Fellowship and the Bess Hokin Prize, and has published poetry under the name Alissa Leigh.

M.A. Vizsolyi
Philadelphia, Pa., U.S.
A professor of creative writing at Purchase College and Goddard College, M.A. Vizsolyi's *The Lamp with Wings: Love Sonnets* (2011) was chosen for the National Poetry Series. Vizsolyi's has also authored two chapbooks, *Notes on Melancholia* (2013) and *The Case of Jane: A Verse Play* (2012).

Derek Walcott (1930–2017)
Castries, Saint Lucia
Born on the former British colony of Saint Lucia, Derek Walcott's work often concerns itself with the intricacies of colonialism and postcolonialism. Walcott's recognition includes a Nobel Prize in Literature, a MacArthur Foundation "genius" award, a Royal Society of Literature Award, and the Queen's Medal for Poetry. He was a professor of poetry at the University of Essex.

G.C. Waldrep
South Boston, Va., U.S.
G.C. Waldrep received a BA from Harvard University, a PhD in history from Duke University, and an MFA from the University of Iowa. His poetry collections include *Goldbeater's Skin* (2003), *Disclamor* (2007), and *Archicembalo* (2009), and he has edited, with Ilya Kaminsky, *Homage to Paul Celan* (2011) and, with Joshua Corey, *The Arcadia Project* (2012).

Kary Wayson
Hanover, N.H., U.S.
Kary Wayson's work has appeared in *Crazyhorse, Poetry Northwest, Alaska Quarterly Review, Filter, The Best American Poetry 2007*, and the 2010 Pushcart Prize anthology. Her debut collection, *American Husband*, was published in 2009.

Eleanor Wilner
Cleveland, Ohio, U.S.
Poet and editor Eleanor Wilner's work has appeared in more than thirty anthologies. She received her BA from Goucher College and a PhD from Johns Hopkins University. Wilner's work often engages a "cultural memory"—including politics and history—instead of the self, and she was actively involved in the Civil Rights movement.

Christian Wiman
Abilene, Texas, U.S.
Poet, translator, editor, and essayist Christian Wiman's 2010 poetry collection *Every Riven Thing* (2010) was named one of the *New Yorker*'s top eleven poetry books of the year. Wiman has taught at Stanford University, Northwestern University, Lynchburg College, and Yale Divinity School, and served as the editor of *Poetry* from 2003 to 2013.

Adam Zagajewski
Lvov, Poland
Considered one of the "New Wave" writers in Poland, Adam Zagajewski's early work was often protest poetry. A recipient of a Guggenheim Fellowship, Zagajewski has also published memoir and prose. In 2010, he was nominated for the Nobel Prize in Literature.

Ghassan Zaqtan
Beit Jala, Palestine
Ghassan Zaqtan spent his childhood in refugee camps as a result of his father's work with the United Nations Relief and Works Agency. From 1978 to 1982, he lived in Beirut, where he published his first collection of poetry. Granted asylum in Damascus after the Israeli-Lebanese War, he then returned to Palestine in 1994, and was awarded the National Medal of Honor by Palestinian president Mahmoud Abbas in 2013.

About the Editors

Ilya Kaminsky was born in Odessa, Ukraine, and currently lives in San Diego. He's the author of *Dancing in Odessa*, and the co-editor of *The Ecco Anthology of International Poetry*. With Jean Valentine, he has co-translated *Dark Elderberry Branch: Poems of Marina Tsvetaeva*.

Dominic Luxford was raised on a sheep farm in the Appalachian Mountains of Virginia, and currently lives in San Francisco. He edited *The McSweeney's Book of Poets Picking Poets*, has been *The Believer* magazine's poetry editor since 2007, and co-founded the McSweeney's Poetry Series.

Jesse Nathan was born in Berkeley, grew up on a wheat farm in Kansas, and lives now in San Francisco. He's the author of several chapbooks, including *Cloud 9*, and is a co-founding editor of the McSweeney's Poetry Series. He's working on a PhD in poetry and poetics at Stanford.

About *Poetry International*

In the Shape of a Human Body I Am Visiting the Earth: Poems from Far and Wide functions as the double issue (#24) of the award-winning international literary journal *Poetry International*, one of the oldest continually running annuals dedicated solely to poetry and poetics from around the world.

Every year, *Poetry International* brings out a book of 400–600 pages of poetry, described by poet and translator Fady Joudah as "diving for pearls in pearl-infested waters." In addition to publishing new work by literary heavyweights, such as Nobel Laureates Tomas Tranströmer, Derek Walcott, and Seamus Heaney, the journal has "discovered" many new voices who, since their appearances in *Poetry International*, have become literary stars. Dunya Mikhail—in particular her poem included here, "The War Works Hard"—was one of many such discoveries. First published in *Poetry International*, the piece later became the title poem of her celebrated collection from New Directions, and has since been translated into many languages.

Poetry International also shares contemporary poetry with underserved youth in San Diego–area schools and community centers through its Poetic Youth writing and arts program. Many of the poems in this book have been read with youth in those communities. When the journal editors taught a poetry class at the Sudanese-American Youth Center, young kids—survivors of war—performed poems from this volume with such force and abandon that our editors knew that our editorial reading process and knowledge of what poetry is—what it can do to a human, as well as to a human voice—will never be the same. We hope this book shares with you some of the passion for poetry that these young readers have shared with us.